Successful
SMALL FOOD GARDENS

Louise Riotte

A Garden Way Publishing Book

STOREY

Storey Communications, Inc.
Schoolhouse Road
Pownal, Vermont 05261

Copyright © 1993 Storey Communications, Inc.

Published by Storey Communications, Inc., Schoolhouse Rd., Pownal, Vermont 05261. Originally published as *Success with Small Food Gardens* in 1977.

Edited by Sandra Webb and Kathleen Bond Borie
Cover design by Meredith Maker
Cover photograph by Cynthia McFarland
Text design and production by Michelle Arabia
Line drawings by the author, except where noted
Indexed by Nan N. Badgett

Printed in the United States by The Book Press
First Printing, January 1993

The information in this book is true and complete to the best of our knowledge. All recommendations are made without guarantee on the part of the author or Storey Communications, Inc. The author and publisher disclaim any liability in connection with the use of this information. For additional information, please contact Storey Communications, Inc., Schoolhouse Road, Pownal, Vermont 05261.

Garden Way Publishing was founded in 1973 as part of the Garden Way Incorporated Group of Companies, dedicated to bringing gardening information and equipment to as many people as possible. Today the name "Garden Way Publishing" is licensed to Storey Communications, Inc., in Pownal, Vermont. For a complete list of Garden Way Publishing titles call 1-800-827-8673. Garden Way Incorporated manufactures products in Troy, New York, under the Troy-Bilt® brand including garden tillers, chipper/shredders, mulching mowers, sicklebar mowers, and tractors. For information on any Garden Way Incorporated product, please call 1-800-345-4454.

Library of Congress Cataloging-in-Publication Data

Riotte, Louise.
    Successful small food gardens / by Louise Riotte.
          p.   cm.
    Rev. ed. of: Success with small food gardens. c1977.
    Includes bibliographical references (p.   ) and index.
    ISBN 0-88266-819-6 (hc) — ISBN 0-88266-818-8 (pbk.)
      1. Vegetable gardening.   2. Organic gardening.   3. Fruit-culture.   4. Edible landscaping.   I. Riotte, Louise. Success with small food gardens.   II. Title.
    SB324.3.R56   1993
    635—dc20   92-53270
                    CIP

Contents

Introduction

A Guide to Intensive Gardening

Y ou want the taste thrills, the joy and rewards of growing your own garden-fresh vegetables, yet all the space you have is a bit of backyard area not occupied by house, garage, and driveway. Don't give up!

For too long, backyard gardening has been neglected in favor of several acres on a homestead or farm. I'm going to do my best to cure that lonely, left-out feeling you've had every time you've picked up a book on gardening. You're going to be surprised and delighted at how much you can produce in a very small space.

And you won't need to give up entirely a lawn and flowers. By the clever use of decorative vegetables in your flowerbeds, you *still* can have roses. In fact, many vegetables, such as onions of all sorts, assist roses by protecting them against black spot. Parsley, too, which is highly attractive as well as deliciously edible, protects roses against beetles.

Reversing this idea, you can use marigolds in your garden to help discourage nematodes, which attack potatoes, strawberries, and various bulbs. Tomatoes interplanted with marigolds grow and produce better than they would alone. Marigolds planted with beans help protect against the Mexican bean beetle. If you want cut flowers for the house, grow extras. Nasturtiums planted with squash keep away squash bugs and improve the growth and flavor of neighboring crops.

If you've been buying all your vegetables at the supermarket, you'll have a real taste surprise when you grow your own: Commercial varieties are primarily grown not for taste but for durability because they often must be shipped long distances. Tender, succulent vegetables have skins that bruise easily, making them poor shippers, yet these are often the most flavorsome. And many of the vegetables that deteriorate quickly are the ones most easily digested and good for you. You can grow these better varieties in your home garden, pick them at their peak of quality, and enjoy all the health benefits.

Of course, one reason for the tremendous surge of interest in home gardening has been the leaping prices of market produce. Another reason is increasing concern about food safety because of all the chemicals that are often a part of large-scale food production. Equally important, to my mind, are matters of taste and nutrition. When you taste the first vegetables you've grown yourself, you'll become aware of the flavor gap between them and those that are store-bought. Freshness alone makes a tremendous difference. Even a poor-flavored variety just

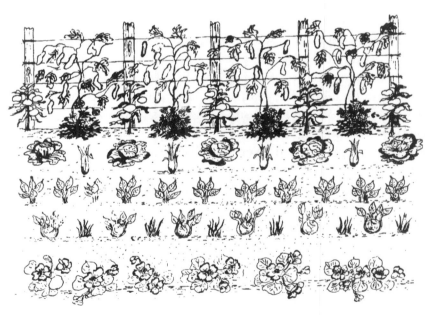

In the garden, as on the table, vegetables and flowers make good companions. Front (and southerly) row, nasturtiums; second row, kohlrabi and chives; third row, beets; fourth row, cabbage and onions; fifth row, tomatoes with marigolds; and in back, climbing cucumbers.

picked from your garden tastes better than the best-flavored variety that has gone through the slow chain from farm to supermarket and often traveled hundreds of miles for many days.

Growing methods influence both flavor and nutritional qualities, too. This has much to do with succulence — the crisp and crunchy texture of carrots, lettuce, onions, radishes, and many other vegetables — or the right "body" for tomatoes, which should be firm but not hard when vine-ripened to its peak. It's easy to get this old-fashioned crispness and flavor: Grow your own!

And the home gardener has an enormous number of varieties from which to choose, varieties that will do well for the home gardener but not for the commercial grower. Choosing varieties carefully may even help you avoid problems. According to William J. Park of the Park Seed Company, "The breeding of new varieties is being aimed in general toward earliness, so that you can get away from many of the disease problems that come later in the season."

Yes, timing is very important, and I concentrate on late crops. In my own garden, for instance, late-planted squash is entirely free of squash bugs. Cauliflower and Chinese celery cabbage, which refuse to head up well in the spring and early summer, produce magnificently in the cool days of fall.

Another consideration for the home gardener is preservatives. Almost everything we buy has been treated chemically to preserve it or hold it as long as possible in marketable condition. Squash, cucumbers, and rutabagas dipped in wax look artificial and taste the same. Synthetics of all sorts are commonly used to boost size, color, and quantity — but not taste. Have you bitten into a commercially grown peach or apricot lately? Most of these fruits and vegetables lack not only flavor and texture but, most important, some of the vitamins and minerals necessary for health.

That's right — health and beauty are still other factors that make growing your own worthwhile. You don't have to settle for chemically sprayed, watery fruits and vegetables if you garden. There also is the physical fitness that comes from this outdoor activity. And you will find that gardening is one of the most fascinating, healthful activities you have ever entered into — it's fun, rewarding, and satisfying.

Here is another aspect from which the home garden should be considered: It still is one of the best nonmonetary ways by which you can accumulate "wealth." The "profits" from your garden are not taxed, and this appeals to the many who are anxious to do more for themselves without being penalized for additional income. And the profit from your garden is just this — a second income on which you owe no tax.

Can you do all this on a small city lot? Yes; others have done and are doing so, and more will be carrying out the idea in the future. If you have *no* space, consider renting a garden plot. (There is more on this later, at the end of Chapter 3.)

Nevertheless, we must be fair. There is no miracle formula by which to have enough superior fruits and vegetables. Superiority presupposes an advance preparation for soil fertility, including the addition of plenty of organic matter and such natural mineral additives as a soil test may indicate are needed.

Many gardeners attempt to work with soil that just won't support a vegetable garden, and stumpy carrots, stringy beets, and bitter lettuce are the result. Your usable soil may even be practically nonexistent — a shallow layer of rocks or hardpan, a heavy clay, or some other combination that's almost impossible to use as a growing medium. In such a situation, try growing plants *above* the soil in a raised bed 12 to 16 inches high — and this solution need not be confined to the backyard. The bed should be placed wherever adequate sun or prevailing winds dictate, or where such a bed (or beds) may fit best in your overall landscape plan or be most convenient. A small kitchen-door salad garden can be quite wonderful for producing special gourmet treats. With such an easily accessible garden, you can dash out often for a handful of fresh herbs for your salad or a few sprigs of mint for lemonade. Plant this little garden very close to your kitchen door.

In Chapter 7, I go further into the matter of soil preparation, which I believe is necessary and vital for intensive gardening. It is the basis of all successful gardening, whether you intend to garden above or below the soil. Right now we will explore the many practical possibilities for increasing production in a small area. Rather than telling you *what* to do, I believe this book can serve best by showing examples of the various ways these things may be accomplished and letting you choose for yourself.

You make the decisions. Retain as much land as you wish for lawn and flowerbeds, and allocate as little (or as much) to your vegetable garden, fruit trees, and nut trees. Remember that beauty and utility can be mixed with happy results. For example, hedges may be edible. Borders need not only be of flowers — why not plant strawberries? Or, if you feel you just *must* have flowers, why not grow some of the many edible kinds? (See Chapter 11 for more about edible flowers.)

What Is a Garden Worth?

This 25-by-15 foot garden should yield most of an average-sized family's vegetables for a year. Use the chart that follows to compare the cost of a packet of seed with the current cost per pound of the vegetable. (Out-of-season vegetables are much higher, of course.) There are other variables, such as the amount you may need to spend for plants and fertilizer, whether you spade up the plot or rent a tiller, and how much water you may use if the season is dry. For a true estimate, these other costs should be subtracted from the total.

Vegetable	Spacing of Row	Yield
Bean (2 plantings)	2 ft.	25 lbs.
Beet (2 plantings)	1 ft.	36 lbs.
Broccoli (hybrid) followed by	2 ft.	24 heads
Cauliflower		12 heads
Cabbage (2 plantings)	2 ft.	24 heads
Carrot (2 plantings)	1 ft.	36 lbs.
Chard	1½ ft.	48 lbs.
Cucumber (hybrid) 6 plants on fence	2 ft.	60 cucumbers
Leek	½ ft.	23 bunches
Lettuce (2 plantings)	1½ ft.	48 heads
Green onion (sets)	½ ft.	24 bunches
Parsley	1 ft.	48 bunches
Pea followed by	2 ft.	15 lbs.
Brussels sprout (hybrid)		60 pts.
Bell pepper (hybrid) 9 plants	2 ft.	40 lbs.
Radish (2 plantings)	1 ft.	24 bunches
Spinach (2 plantings)	1 ft.	12 lbs.
Tomato (hybrid) 9 plants, wire circles	2 ft.	100 lbs.
Zucchini (hybrid) 5 plants	2 ft.	40 lbs.

How you care for your garden also affects savings. Plants that are kept well picked keep producing and are prevented from going to seed. Mulched plants require less weeding and need less water. Cucumbers and tomatoes trellised or staked not to sprawl over other plants and zucchini kept in bounds increase yields. Vegetables in raised beds may be planted more closely.

Fences serve as supports for many climbing plants, but you can also have vine towers in your garden that conserve space by training plants upward. Don't forget that good soil fertility allows you to put many more plants in a small space.

So far I haven't even mentioned the vegetable varieties particularly adapted to the small garden — the midgets — that most nurseries and seed catalogs now list. Midgets are available for almost every category (corn, cabbage, tomato, lettuce, cucumber, muskmelon, carrot, eggplant, squash, radish, bean, pea, baby beet, and even watermelon) and many are of superior quality and taste. (Read more about midget vegetables in Chapter 4.) And, as in larger gardens, you also may want herbs, which take little room and are helpful as well to other vegetables and fruits because of their protective qualities.

Don't forget those other important dwarfs — the fruit trees — which now come in sizes suitable for even the smallest property. They are extremely productive, and the full-sized fruits are as tasty as those of

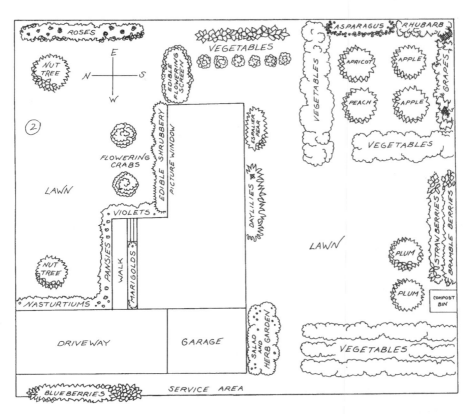

A plan for landscaping an interior lot where the house is located near the front.

standard varieties. (There's more on dwarf fruit trees in Chapter 9.)

All of the space-saving techniques will be explored and evaluated later in Chapter 3. But first, each separate homesite use must be considered carefully in its relation to the overall plan and space allocated for each outdoor living area to contribute to comfort, convenience, and pleasure. To do this effectively, there must first be order and organization and thought given to the placement of each necessary element.

CHAPTER 1

Plan a Practical Landscape

Many of us want to use our yards both as outdoor living areas that provide privacy and entertaining space and as a source for garden-fresh produce. So, landscaping means designing the garden areas not only for beauty but also for comfort and practicality. It means consideration of walls, fences, or hedges for privacy as well as of prevailing winds for climate control.

Careful planning of a garden area is an important preliminary step to its development and construction. Before even planning where to put vegetable beds, the first step should be the completion of overall design and choice of the kinds, the general arrangement, and the locations of plants to be used. And, a little foresight may be money in the bank: Changing the position of trees, shrubs, and garden beds and altering such basic features as paths, terraces, and steps can be very expensive once the work has been accomplished — but on paper it is easy and costs nothing.

You may have to live a long time with the landscape you design. So, take sufficient time and give adequate thought to developing a plan that is just right for the size of your property and convenient and compatible with your own life-style, which may be entirely different from that of your next-door neighbor.

Even before you plan on paper, it's a good idea to look around and see what others have done with properties of a size similar to your own. Familiarize yourself with the various kinds of plants that thrive in your locality (and that are offered for sale by local nurseries). If there are parks, botanical gardens, or other public plantings in your vicinity, these may also help you in deciding what to grow. Note the size and appearance of these plants after they have grown for several years and are approaching maturity. It is quite important that you visualize how large your trees and shrubs eventually may be.

Much can be done even when the problems are compounded by existing trees, shrubs, hedges, or fences — perhaps some on adjacent properties. If they are on your own land, you must decide what to keep and what to remove or replace.

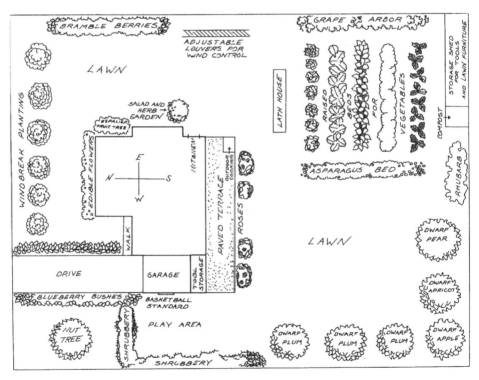

In this plan the house is smaller and nearer the street, allowing more planting areas.

Begin With a Good Design

In general, simplicity should be favored, and above all, don't attempt to do too much all at once. With a definite site plan, trees and shrubs may be added a few at a time, spreading the cost over a period of years. This will be easier on you, as will their care.

At the beginning, don't construct rock gardens or other major features that you may find later don't fit well into your landscape. Avoid introducing twists and curves into paths unnecessarily. You may decide that a small vegetable garden carefully planted, well weeded, and well watered is even more productive and fits in more attractively than a larger one that is neglected.

Unfortunately, there are few places where the lot owner has complete control over all factors affecting the design, which is often dictated by the lot's shape, soil, and exposures; the house's location; possible outcrops of rock; and existing trees on the property itself or on neighboring land. Sometimes a number of these features can be changed to improve the design, but sometimes the changes may prove to be too expensive and the design must be woven around them. If this happens, don't despair. Necessary compromises quite often result in a more attractive design than you would have believed possible.

Stay With Your Plan

Once you have decided on your landscaping scheme, stay with it and let your garden and plantings mature. This doesn't mean that you are limited to the existing plan. You can always modify within your general framework and still experiment in plant selection.

A homesite is never static: Each year you will see important changes in the growth of trees and shrubs, and these changes will govern the scale of later planting from year to year. Sometimes the growth of a tree (and its increasing shade and roots) damages nearby shrubs or less vigorous trees. If you know this may happen, consider the use of shrubs as trees. Take time to browse at your local nurseries. Find out the requirements of a shrub or tree and then decide whether, where, and how you could use it effectively. Trees may also be lost through storm or disease, and this may cause a radical change in your garden design.

A home landscape design is never really finished. You should develop a watchful eye so you know when to remove trees and shrubs to prevent overcrowding, when to remove a branch to improve a window view, or whether to add a little more color in one place to balance color in another.

Before you introduce new plants, ask yourself if they will help or hurt the overall effect of the surrounding, established plants and whether they will thrive and look well in future years. As you study the plants that do well in your own particular area, these determinations become increasingly easier.

Simple Principles Are Best

First, always assess what you have before planning what you would like to do. To create a pleasing overall design, you need to understand the underlying principles of design — unity, balance, proportion, and variety. Unity gives the feeling that everything is right and belongs together, balance focuses attention on a center of interest, proportion gives a feeling of restfulness, and variety prevents monotony.

For instance, if you plant a large tree directly in front of your house, the house and the tree will compete for interest. But if the tree is placed a little to one side, it will seem to frame the house and provide visual unity.

Applying Design Principles

Always strive for balance. A high, heavy planting on one side and a low one on the other creates a lack of balance and proportion and makes your planting look incomplete. Too much thick, massive foliage overpowers your house, but if all the plants are small, then the house appears too dominant.

Symmetry exists when the design is the same on both sides, but a balance in landscape planting can be attained in other ways. A tall, lacy, and open tree may be balanced by a smaller but denser and coarser one. Two small trees may balance a larger one. Two small crabapple trees that frame a picture window may be balanced with a larger nut tree planted on the opposite side of the house.

You can achieve variety by the use of different types of plant materials. Differences in shape, size, texture, density, line, and color add interest to your planting yet must be carefully combined so that they blend harmoniously.

To achieve our objectives, utility as well as beauty must be considered in the plantings chosen. Of course, it may be desirable in some locations to use plants that are not edible (such as evergreens), but even these can be useful as screens or supports for other plants that may need protection.

Consider also convenience. The simplest solutions are apt to be the ones that are the most orderly and also the most useful (such as having a tiny salad and herb garden next to the kitchen door).

Your House

The house itself should always be considered the focal point and center of interest, and the landscape plan should emphasize its good points and minimize any less attractive ones. The house should seem to be an integral part of the landscape, as if it "grew" there naturally, and not look like an isolated component. Everything, right to the very edges of your property, including the house, lawn, trees, shrubs, and flowers, should be a part of the pattern. Foundation plantings, properly planned, serve to "tie" the house to the ground. But, be careful! Those dainty young trees or shrubs may grow to overpower the house, to compete with it for interest, or even to shut out the sunlight.

I can't give hard-and-fast rules for developing an individual property because no two are exactly alike. Growing things, too, are ever-changing in shape and size, and although pruning and clipping help to keep them in proportion, you should know the size your chosen plants will be when fully mature.

Studying Your Site. The path of the sun and its intensity through the seasons of the year and the hours of the day also determine the kind of plants you grow and affect their location. If the number of warm, sunny days you can count on is limited, you should give this important consideration, especially in planning the locations of your vegetable gardens, because you should place them where they receive the most sunlight. However, if summer temperatures are high, you may wish to plan for overhead structures to filter the sunlight or screens of foliage to shade certain plants from the hot western sun.

Remember also that nowhere in North America is the sun ever directly overhead. This means that a tree or an overhead structure never casts all of its shade directly beneath itself. So, in planning the location of your vegetable plots, it is important to consider the effects of any

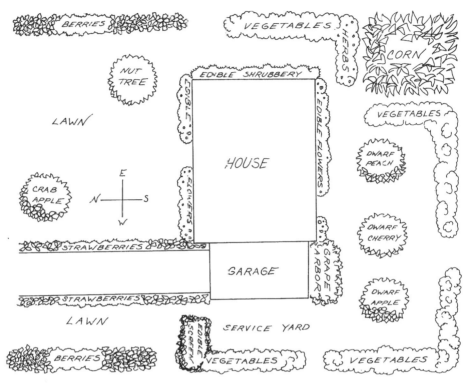

Raised garden beds are used in this design as a decorative part of the overall plan.

nearby shade trees, which may be beneficial if located west or north of your gardens, but disastrous if located south or east.

Prevailing Winds. The prevailing wind is the one that blows most often. A careful study of the wind pattern around your house and lot will pay off handsomely. And when I say "careful," I mean just that, for prevailing winds differ from place to place according to geographical area. They are usually westerly (blow from the west) throughout North America and much of western Europe.

However, the prevailing wind does not blow continually. Winds from other directions frequently occur. Summer's prevailing wind may not be the same as winter's. And the wind is never steady, but blows in a series of gusts and lulls. A more realistic measure of wind is its average over a longer period.

The prevailing wind in the area where you live can be very important in its effect on outdoor comfort, home heating, and gardening success. Narrow this down a little more by studying the wind pattern around your house and over your lot. Plan your outdoor relaxation area with this in mind because too much wind blowing across it on a cool day can be as unpleasant as no breeze at all on a warm one. Plan the placement of your vegetable garden and fruit trees with the prevailing wind in mind, too. In the small area of your own lot, you can control the wind and modify it to suit your needs by the use of fences, screens, or plants.

You can determine the generally prevailing wind from the direction of "lean" of the trees on surrounding properties. But, bear in mind that the direction of the wind around your own house may not be quite the same as that of the house next door. Wind flows like water, eddying, twisting, and breaking into several currents as it spills over and around obstacles.

In checking the wind around your home, remember that even though the house itself is likely to be your biggest windbreak, some additions may be needed to be effective. When the wind is strong, it may spill over the housetop and drop on the opposite side's outdoor living area. A solid obstacle is not always the most efficient one, for wind will wash over it much as a stream of water does over a solid barrier.

A solid fence to screen the wind is more effective if you leave an open space at the bottom. The greatest protection is at a distance equal to the height of the fence. Although a slatted fence may be less desirable from the viewpoint of privacy, it gives better control than a solid one, and a very strong wind is less likely to blow it down. A louvered fence provides the best protection over the greatest distance, because the reversed louvers direct wind away from the area you want to protect.

In northern areas, living fences are effective windbreaks. A planting of evergreens on the side of the prevailing wind may save on fuel bills in winter and give additional privacy to an outdoor living area in summer. On the other hand, deciduous trees are natural air conditioners: Transpiration of their leaves both makes their surroundings cooler and provides welcome shade in summer.

The Path to Your Door. The appearance of the approach to your front door is important, particularly on a small lot where space is at a premium. It is usually best to let the path run straight to the house, although on a lot of unusual shape, a gracefully curved path may be preferable both for utility and beauty. If a straight path would cut the lawn into long rectangles quite unequal in area, it is better to have the path run alongside the driveway and make a right-angled turn near the house.

You also should consider the width of the walk and any problems of construction, drainage, or cost. The path may need to be fitted to a slope or may require steps if there is a terrace. Choose material that is in keeping with your type of house. You may decide to plant a tree to shade the walk and to frame the entrance. A border of flowers or small fruits is a part of the whole pattern, too.

Your Very Own Plot of Land

Homesites usually are either an interior (middle-of-the-block) lot or a corner lot. Each type has attractive features as well as problems. Another type of site is the pie- or wedge-shaped lot. My own lot happens to be of this shape and on a corner. Planning for privacy as well as harmony in the design has taken much thought.

A corner lot does present a difficult problem when you are attempting to achieve the maximum in private space. Compared with an interior lot, where you need give up only the setback space on the front, a corner lot may need special treatment on the sides as well.

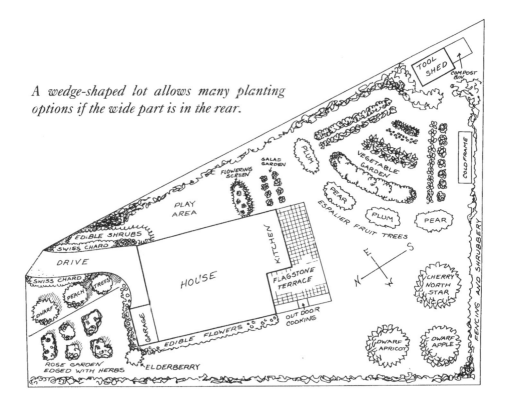

A wedge-shaped lot allows many planting options if the wide part is in the rear.

What you can do may depend to some extent on local ordinances. Before adding trees, shrubs, hedges, or fences to create more private and usable outdoor space between your house and those of your neighbors or the street, it is essential to find out the distances allowed. Plantings sometimes obscure traffic and are considered accident hazards. If there are legal restrictions about corner plantings, it is best to find this out in advance. Even so, many find a corner lot desirable. Although some private space is lost, there still remains a unique feeling of openness.

An interior lot is most likely to be a rectangular shape of clearly defined space. It may be broad and short or long and narrow. With this type of lot, even more than with one on a corner, you need to note what your neighbors have planted, especially if there are any large trees.

You also should consider the view of (and from) neighboring roofs and windows. Your own landscape planning may be influenced by as many as four or five neighboring yards and houses. Even so, in landscaping for privacy you need not be entirely controlled by the geometric shape of your lot to the point that you plant only around the edges. You may find that introducing curves into the landscape is an excellent way to overcome the rectangular feeling.

Although it would seem that the pie- or wedge-shaped lot would present the most problems, this need not be the case. If well planned, this shape may even be the most interesting and desirable of all, especially if the narrow end is toward the street. A lot so situated has the least space on the street, and the large backyard can be divided into several garden or service areas that work together in a unifying effect.

Planning Your Space Requirements. The design of your outdoor living and service areas is determined by the space available, your individual preference, and your family's needs. A family with children may wish to provide more recreation space than one whose children are grown. Plan a play area that can be changed to other uses as your children grow up. A small space for a sandbox, a play yard, or a portable swimming pool may be enlarged in time to accommodate tricycles or bicycles; later on, you may wish to eliminate this area altogether.

A game area is desirable for a family that enjoys playing outdoors; if possible, let your driveway do double duty by mounting a basketball hoop over the garage door, or let this area serve for other games, such as volleyball or badminton.

A patio, even a small one, is a definite bonus for most families. If it has a paved, level surface on which to set chairs and a table, no longer need the legs poke holes in the lawn. A properly planned patio is subject to neither too much sun or wind nor evenings that are too chilly. You also may wish to plan space here for container plants and a barbecue grill.

If an outdoor clothesline is needed, it should be placed close to the utility area but screened from the patio and, if possible, from the main garden or windows as well.

Gardening and other tools may be stored in your garage if space permits, but you may decide to add a small shed set off in a corner of the garden with its outlines camouflaged by a planting of shrubs, vines, or both. A shed provides storage space for garden tools, lawn mower, watering equipment, garden cart, peat moss, fertilizer, and lawn furniture.

A compost bin, that essential to good gardening, also may be rendered inconspicuous in much the same manner as the outdoor storage shed. For a small property it need not be large, but it should be at least 4 by 5 feet.

The most important planning of all is to allow adequate space for your food garden, which may take the form of several raised beds situated to fit best for sun, shade, and watering facilities and to be attractive parts of the overall landscape design.

I feel, too, that even the smallest lot should make room for a cold frame (more details on this at the end of Chapter 2), lathhouse, or greenhouse. This can be as large or as small as your space allows, but a special place for starting vegetable and flower plants is of tremendous convenience and permits quick replacement of plants as they are spent or used so that vacancies in the garden are of short duration.

If you have your heart set on a decorative feature for your garden, a birdbath could be appealing while also attracting birds that help with insect pests. Of course, a small pool or fountain also would be great if you have the room and an available water supply.

Planning for Utility Connections. Sillcocks or outdoor water connections of some type should be a part of every garden plan. Even in regions where rainfall is adequate, it may not occur at the right times. Watering of vegetables is critical at every stage of growth if they are to achieve the superiority for which we are aiming. Newly planted shrubs and trees also have particular water needs for the first year or two until they become established.

It is always best and least expensive to plan for the water connections and system when a house is built. The cost of putting in an irrigation system at a later date may be almost prohibitive.

The location of sewer pipes or septic tank drains should also be considered when planting trees and shrubs. When you are buying a property, check to see whether water outlets are placed so that future connection to them is possible without cutting through lawns or pavement. If you are building, you may wish to plan for a winter-draining water faucet in the garden work area and connections for sprinkler systems. And, water isn't the only consideration. You may like to light your patio at night or use an electric mower or clippers. If so, plan for outdoor electrical outlets.

Selecting Your Homesite

For most people, the landscaping problem means working with a house already built and plantings already present. However, others buy property on which the house is yet to be built. With a bare lot there is no need to consider discarding existing plantings and starting over with an entirely new design. A vacant lot gives you the best chance to decide what type of landscaping is best adapted to your family's needs and likes. When there is a choice of lots with large trees, their species, location, and condition are important. Be aware of the tree species that are subject to diseases in your area, for later removal is expensive.

How Does Your Soil Drain? A successful garden depends in part on the type of soil you have. And although I shall discuss soil improvement in Chapter 7, let's consider here the type of soil you have.

Of course, the ideal soil should drain well while still retaining moisture and nutrients. Heavy soil usually drains too slowly, a light one too fast. Either extreme can be improved with quantities of organic matter.

A shallow soil that is underlain with a compacted material impervious to water and roots should have the impenetrable layer removed. But, if it is impractical to dig this layer out because of its depth, it may be better to bring in soil and garden in raised beds.

Steeply sloping lots are more difficult and expensive to develop and maintain than level ones. However, a moderate slope up from the road often gives a pleasant setting. A slope to the south adds growing days — a bonus for gardeners in the north.

Even a natural feature, such as a rocky outcrop or a small brook, may

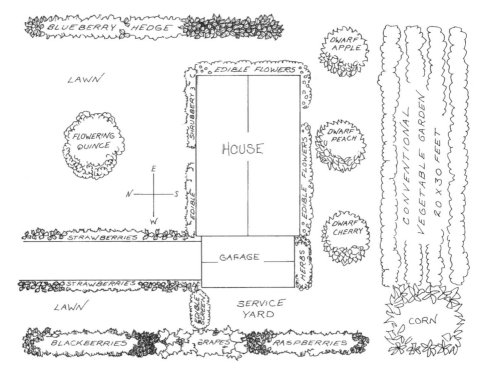

This is another arrangement for the same house lot shown earlier but with placement of a conventional 20 x 30-foot garden at the back.

be a special asset to the site. However, any unusual feature should be carefully considered, for if it is not desirable, the expense of eliminating it may be too great.

Drainage is a very important factor. A lot that is lower than its neighbors or the street may be flooded and become a recurring expense and a discouragement, if not completely impossible for gardening. Find out if there is a soil and drainage map available from the seller or the city engineer's office. This will give you a head start in assessing the problem and planning your layout.

If there is no drainage problem, don't unwittingly cause one by landscaping across the natural drainage and thereby obstructing the flow of water away from the house. A large expanse of concrete or brick, if not properly installed, may choke off surface drainage, as happened to our property a few years ago. To facilitate turning our travel trailer, we laid down a slab of concrete. The first hard rain made a lake of our backyard, the water flowed under the house, and only quick pumping

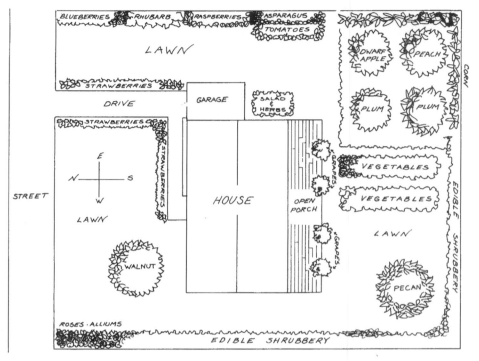

This house centered on a small lot suggests border plantings, small beds, and trees.

saved the floor furnace from permanent damage. Drain tile cured the situation, and we have had no further trouble.

If a drainage problem occurs after additional construction, a shallow gravel-filled trench along the edge may be sufficient to divert water into safer channels. Lead the ditch to drainage channels along your fence at the side of your lot. If downspout water is a problem, get a canvas roll-out hose.

Laying drain tile is expensive and laborious, but it is also the most permanent way to avoid or to cure a drainage problem. If you decide to use drain tile, lay it on a sloping gravel bed, leaving a small space between tiles, or use perforated pipe. Cover the tile with gravel, then with polyethylene plastic sheeting, and lastly with soil.

Although a great deal of stress is given to water drainage, air drainage is equally important in gardening, and it may not be thought of until a problem becomes apparent. Just as water flows down a slope, so does cold air, and because it is heavier than warm air, it displaces the warm air and accumulates in hollows and valleys. When this happens, plots at the bottoms of slopes are likely to experience lower temperatures, which will last longer than those at the higher elevations.

Therefore, low-lying sites should be avoided for plants on the borderline of tenderness as well as for fruit and other early-flowering trees and shrubs that might have their blossoms destroyed by a late spring frost. Fruit blossoms often are damaged on these low-lying sites when similar trees planted higher are spared.

Putting Your Plan on Paper

Secure a plot plan from the seller or city engineer's office, if possible: It will save you a great deal of time and work. If you cannot obtain one, you need to measure and compass-orient the lot, the house structure with its doors and windows, and all other existing features, such as walks, garage and driveway, trees, and flowerbeds.

- ❦ As a guideline, use a straight line of known length and compass direction, such as the front line of the house or the street front, as your base. (Remember that in some regions a compass shows considerable variation from true north and that you must adjust for this.)

- ❦ Put in all the straight lines parallel to this guideline first and then add those at right angles. Locate trees in relation to these more easily measured features.

- ❦ Sketch in irregular lines of shrub beds and borders next with fair accuracy. Then, consider any objects on nearby property that you want to screen or a view that you may wish to emphasize. If there are large trees close to your lot on a neighboring property or on city-owned frontage, they should also be indicated.

- ❦ Note the direction of prevailing winds throughout the year.

- ❦ The location of easements that may affect your planning, such as underground telephone lines and trunk sewers, should be plotted in.

- ❦ Check with your city engineer or local building officials about restrictions (if any) on the height and placement of fences and attached or detached structures.

- ❧ When you have gathered all the detailed information possible about your particular lot, it is time to transcribe it in detail onto graph paper.

- ❧ Use a large sheet of graph paper and show in detail exactly what you have to work with. Draw to the largest scale your paper allows (usually ¼ inch equaling 1 foot). This is your base map.

- ❧ With all the physical restrictions and requirements of your lot clearly noted, bring out the checklist previously made that evaluates your particular needs or preferences.

- ❧ Tape a sheet of clear tracing paper (obtainable at most art supply or stationery stores) over the base map on which you have outlined your house, lot, and other permanent features. You can do this as many times as you like without marring your base map, changing around the various areas and planned uses until you have everything exactly the way you want it to be.

The first time or two you may just have fun, putting things in approximately where you think they should go: plants, trees, fences, windbreaks, or small structures such as a toolshed or a compost bin. Don't approach this planning too seriously. After working on it for a while you will begin to arrive at final decisions.

Experiment with the placement of the various separate areas most important to you and your family (such as the garden or garden beds, tool storage shed, lawn sections, service yard, patio, or play area). After a few attempts you gradually will formulate a design that suits your needs. You may enlarge (or reduce) some areas, eliminate some, or decide on something completely new.

Once the overall plan has been decided, you can begin to get down to specifics and go into greater detail with each area you have included. For instance, you may want just one garden of a conventional type. Or you may want several raised beds placed to best advantage for sun or prevailing winds.

Ask yourself if you have placed the patio in a spot that is too warm or too windy or if you need fencing for climate control or overhead trees for shade. Can you successfully hide the clothesline and the garbage cans in the areas designated and yet have them conveniently situated? Is the play area placed so that you can keep an eye on the children?

You may even want to decide now about the type of lawn you will have, although to some extent this is dictated by the climate and soil of your new home (see Chapter 7).

Whether to fence all or part of your property is another important matter to decide. "Good fences make good neighbors" is an old saying that still is true. Dogs and kids often don't mix well with gardens and flowers.

You also may wish to plan for different types of screening (walls, fences, or plants) to separate the different areas of your yard. Pathways also should be planned carefully and early and situated so that traffic flows easily on them and around your house and garden.

CHAPTER 2

Planning for Vegetables

Adetailed garden plan will save you much time and work. Whether you plan to garden in a conventional, single large plot in the backyard or in several raised beds, you should draw the size of your plot or plots to scale, preferably on graph paper.

Because you may not have room for all the vegetables you like, make a list of those your family prefers and allot them roughly enough space for proper growth. In Chapter 3 you'll learn how to get more yield than normal in small areas. But first, you must decide *where* you want your vegetables to grow and weigh the various possibilities of your site with regard to sun, wind, shade, and other factors.

If you have decided on a conventional-type garden, you may wish to rent or even buy a tiller. If your plot is small, hand work may be better. Either way, one of the first factors to consider is moisture.

Conserve Moisture: Double Digging

A garden has to have moisture. Without it, seeds will not germinate and plants will not grow. If the plants are allowed to dry out, they become tough and stringy and may even die. But there are ways to provide moisture besides watering and irrigation (see Chapter 6). Even though you can't affect the weather, there are ways of controlling some of the rainfall after it hits the ground.

One of the best ways of doing this in a single-plot garden is to trap the fall rains and winter snows, thus raising the level of the soil moisture. In a conventional garden this may be accomplished by temporary terracing. Each fall, bury the refuse from the summer garden along with any other plant residues you can come by. First, remove the topsoil to a depth of approximately 10 inches from a strip 4 feet wide and the width of your garden. Pile this to one side of your excavation. Now, remove the subsoil to the same depth and pile it on the other side. The refuse you have collected is then layered in the ditch. Next, layer in the subsoil (along with some topsoil). Put the rest of the topsoil in last.

This method accomplishes three things: It breaks up the hardpan, mixes a small amount of topsoil with the subsoil (to improve its water retention), and adds organic matter to the soil.

The excavation should always be curved, with the ends slightly farther uphill than the center. Because of the addition of the refuse when refilling and the looseness of the soil, you will end up with a fairly high ridge across the garden. This ridge forms a shallow pocket, catches the rainfall or melting snow as it falls on the garden, and forces it to seep into the soil instead of running off. By spring most of the ridge will have settled, and any remaining elevation can be raked level.

Small-Plot Gardening

The conventional type of garden may be the most desirable on a large lot where there is ample space. However, because so many of today's homes are built on small lots, a more compact type of vegetable garden is becoming popular. To some extent, emphasis is swinging away from quantity production to the direction of experimentation, informality, efficiency, and just plain fun.

Homeowners whose space is limited usually don't want to turn their *entire* yard into a growing ground for vegetables. For them, or for homeowners whose soil is rocky or very heavy, raised gardening beds often prove to be the best possible answer. Raised beds may take several different forms, which I will talk about as I go along.

French Intensive Gardening. This technique, first introduced to the United States in the 1960s by Alan Chadwick at the student gardening project at the University of California, Santa Cruz, also

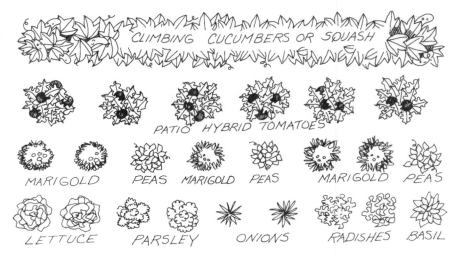

This planting of a narrow bed places tall, climbing vegetables at the north side.

involves double digging. It is very similar to the method that the Chinese have used for centuries to get as much food as possible out of every available square foot of soil.

In intensive gardening, the growing surface must be raised above ground level. Preparing such raised beds means a considerable addition of new materials and labor the first time, but as soil conditions improve, the work becomes progressively easier.

The first step is to stake out your garden area and weed it. Then comes the hardest part. The entire plot is subjected to "double digging." This involves dividing the plot into parallel trenches and loosening and improving the soil. Begin by digging and removing a spade's depth of soil in the first trench. Then a second spade depth of soil is loosened. Follow the same procedures for the next trench, and then add the topsoil from the first trench to the second trench.

Compost or manure, bonemeal, wood ash, or rock fertilizers are now added as the top layer of soil is put back. The inclusion of all this extra material results in a built-up soil, and some means must be provided to hold it in place. You can use whatever is available — old railroad ties, boards, bricks, cement blocks, or native rock — if it is uniform enough to construct a shallow wall. Depending on what you use, this wall can also provide a place to sit later as you work on the bed as well as keep this super-rich soil in place and prevent loss of nutrients when it rains.

As a further benefit, the texture of the built-up soil has greatly improved aeration because the surface and sides are exposed to the air. However, this also may mean that more watering will be necessary because evaporation is increased.

Such exposure and evaporation is more of a drawback in a hot climate than in a cool one. In a cool location, this method has the additional advantage of warming up the soil and drying it out, giving added days of gardening time by enabling the gardener to plant earlier in the spring.

The length of your intensive gardening beds may be determined by personal preference, appearance, or available space. However, the width is very important. The beds should be narrow enough for you to reach the middle when you sit on either side — about 5 feet wide. This is a big advantage over a normal garden: Because the soil is never walked on, it is not compacted and the aeration is not limited. Also, you can cultivate the entire area and need no in-garden paths.

Plant Spacing. Intensive gardening is just that — the plants are placed very close together, providing a "living mulch." By spacing plants so close that their leaves almost touch, the bases of the plants have a protective shade of green leaves above. This layer simultaneously traps moisture between the ground and the leaves and blocks out sunlight from the soil.

Plants, once seeded or set close together, are thinned out as they grow. The leaves almost touch but don't overcrowd each other. The plants' own leaves provide shade while cutting off sunlight for most weeds, thus reducing the need for hand weeding. Usually, only one early-spring weeding is necessary, and the weeds come out easily, roots and all, from the loose, friable soil. Once the vegetables start growing, further weed growth is inhibited.

This system of gardening is most productive if bulky vegetables are omitted. It is particularly useful for growing carrots, onions, lettuce, chives, peas, and Swiss chard. Many other greens such as mustard, kale, and spinach do well, too. Midget vegetables, discussed in Chapter 4, also may be used. Tall-growing vegetables like corn and spreading ones like squash and pumpkins are best placed elsewhere, for they take up too much room to be practical.

The real benefit of this type of gardening comes from the increased number of plants that grow and do well in a given area. In time, you may wish to increase the number of your beds to two or more and practice succession planting so that you have something from your garden every month that your climate permits.

Planning the Beds. If you have access to your garden strips on both sides, they can be as wide as 5 feet. If they are accessible only on one side, a 3-foot width is usually the most comfortable and convenient for reaching.

Intensive gardening beds need not be long rectangles. They can be modified into pleasing L-shaped curves, permitting more attractive landscaping and allowing room for a lawn. Plant taller vegetables like

A plan for a larger garden is based on both intercropping and succession plantings.

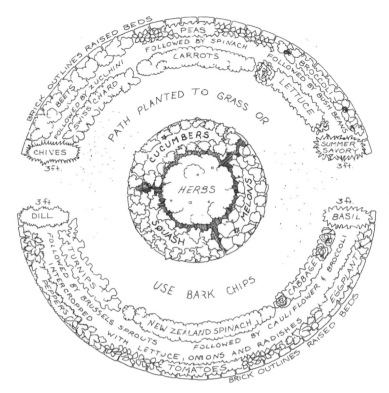

A decorative circular, raised-bed garden keeps producing succession crops through-out the growing year.

okra, peas, and pole beans in the back (north side) followed by a row of tomatoes, peppers, eggplant, and tall herbs. A row of dwarf marigolds could come next, with parsley, bush beans, root, and leaf vegetables in the front (south side). If you plant corn, allow a special space for it and always plant it in a solid block.

If you have always had a conventional type of garden, one of the greatest obstacles to overcome is a psychological one. You must divest yourself of the idea that plants necessarily belong in parallel rows separated by paths. Discipline yourself to grow vegetables in decorative clumps as you do flowers, or by interplanting flowers with vegetables. But, keep a detailed planting plan so you won't forget where everything is!

Remember to allow adequate room for each plant. Experienced gardeners know that the root system usually reflects what grows on top, and if there is space for the crowns, you aren't crowding the roots.

If you have room, you may want to plant a separate bed of perennial vegetables such as asparagus, rhubarb, or Jerusalem artichoke. But, remember that these plants are apt to grow very tall. Asparagus and rhubarb are decorative, but Jerusalem artichoke is a rather coarse plant that should be kept in the back, preferably where it can be tied to a fence, because the plant tends to sprawl as it matures. The tubers are tasty and healthful, but the plant may become a spreading weed if not kept carefully within bounds.

Other perennials that might be added are many types of alliums such as garlic, shallots, multiplier onions, Egyptian or tree onions, and leeks. There are many perennial herbs, too, and a list of these is given in the Appendix.

The Kitchen-Door Salad Garden. If you enjoy cooking and entertaining, this little garden can be a great convenience and earn you an enviable reputation with family and friends. It need not and should not be large, so what you intend to plant there must be given careful thought. Note whether your plot is in sun or shade.

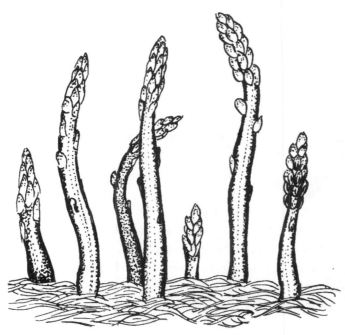

Some of the newer asparagus varieties can be cut as early as the year after planting.

There are many tasty herbs that do well in shade or filtered sunlight; one of these is the almost-indispensable parsley. (There is more about herbs in Chapter 4.) So, why not dig up a small plot near your kitchen door, edge it with stones or boards, add some compost if the soil is poor, and proceed to plant?

My suggestion is to plant at least one of the mints, all of which are very easy to grow. Inside your parsley rim, try some low-growing chives, useful for many dishes, and the patrician shallots, equally easy to grow. Getting a start of shallots may be a bit expensive, but just a few bulbs increase tremendously in a short time, and your first purchase may well be your last.

You might also like to include midget carrots and scallions, dwarf lettuce, and other herbs for seasoning. I find sweet basil to be one of the most useful herbs; if you choose a tall type, put it in the center. Ornamental opal basil is a beautiful, compact, 15-inch-tall plant whose deep purple provides contrast to the green of your other salad garden treasures.

Edging Your Lawn With Vegetables. Of course, you don't want to give up all your lawn space to growing fruits and vegetables. But having both is not the insurmountable problem it may appear to be at

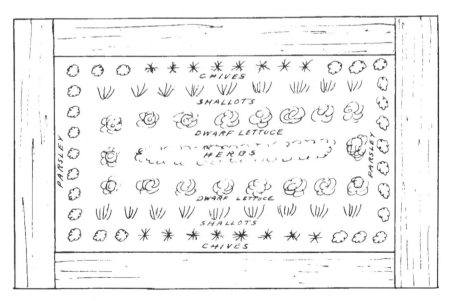

A small raised-bed kitchen garden is fine for herbs and salad greens.

Gardening in Raised Beds

Capsule Information for Starting Vegetables from Seed

Soil: After beds have been dug and soil additives put in, you may have a mound of rough clods. Let the beds air out for a few days. Then, still keeping the mound shape, work the soil until it becomes fine textured. Set some extra soil aside in containers to sprinkle on your seeds.

Fertilizer: At this point, additional fertilizer may be added. Spread on a layer of wood ash, bonemeal, well-rotted manure, or additional compost. Even out this material and work it into the top 3 to 5 inches of the mound.

Water: Soak the soil well the day before planting. Attention must be given to regular watering during the plants' growth. Try to keep the root zones moist, or at least the top 2 inches of soil.

Seed: Sow seed; scatter it as evenly as possible and try not to miss the corners. You may get better coverage if you mix fine seeds with sand.

Cover: Next, cover the seeds with a fine layer of the soil you set aside. Some gardeners get excellent results by covering seeds with a thin layer of peat moss. Remember that seeds need covers of different depths. Beans need as much as 1 inch or more. Small seeds, like carrots, need only ¼ inch.

Sprouts: Most seeds, depending on the variety, should sprout in a few days. If weather is hot, dry, or windy, keep the seed bed moist with a sprinkler can or fine spray. In extremely hot or windy weather it may be necessary to cover seeds for a few days to retain moisture so sprouting can take place. Water as necessary after sprouting. Raised beds tend to dry out more quickly.

Weeds: Weeding thickly planted vegetables in raised beds is minimal, but take care to remove those weeds that do occasionally pop up. Shoulder-to-shoulder plant spacing means that every bit of rich soil produces nutritious edibles, so don't let weeds steal any of the moisture and nutrients. As the vegetables grow, they shade their own root zones and retain soil moisture, allowing almost no weeds to grow.

first. One solution is to use vegetables (and their companion herbs and flowers) as decorative plantings set in beds or borders, just as flower gardens are normally planted.

Border plantings may even save you up to half of the space you would use in a regular garden because you have no need for paths, and you'll have increased yields from your intensive gardening, intercropping, and succession planting.

Just as with raised beds, your "edge garden" benefits from a concentration of soil-building methods. Compost, mulch, and fertilizer are more effective and go farther when placed in compact strips.

Once your soil is in good shape, you may not need to spade or "work" it very often because you will not be compacting it by walking on it. On a rectangular lot you can have garden beds edging your lawn on both sides and at the back of the house, plus additional strips here and there of both flowers and vegetables — just the way you would put in flowerbeds.

One caution regarding beds that edge walks and driveways in very cold areas: Deep frosts and piled, plowed snow may cause plant damage. Put on a heavy, protective mulch in the fall and take it off in the spring, as you do with strawberry beds.

A border next to the house on its southern exposure warms up first in the spring and probably should be the site of your first planting. Climbing snow peas could go in here, with a row or two of beets or spinach in front. Grow the early vegetables for table use and if there is a surplus, plan to can, freeze, or pickle.

It is important that you learn to think in small amounts. With a small-scale project you must plan to can or freeze just a few jars or packages at a time. It doesn't take long to put away a few vegetables each day, and as the season advances, you'll find your storage shelves and freezer filling surprisingly fast.

Build a Garden You Can Reach

Many people, young adults as well as senior citizens, have back problems and can't bend over, so why not bring the gardens up to them? There are several ways of doing this: Build boxes, preferably using redwood lumber 2 feet wide by 4 feet long, and set them on sturdy 2-inch by 4-inch legs at the height most convenient for work. Vary the depths of the boxes according to what you plant, making some 8 inches and others 12 inches deep.

These raised beds have an added advantage: You can place them anywhere you wish (for example, out from under the shade of your or your neighbors' large trees). But, I consider a location near a southern house wall to be the best one.

For the planter boxes to produce well, of course, they must be filled with good garden soil — a sandy loam into which plenty of organic matter (compost or well-decomposed manure) has been added. If you

Edible-pod sugar peas grow like green peas and mature early. Pick when young and cook lightly.

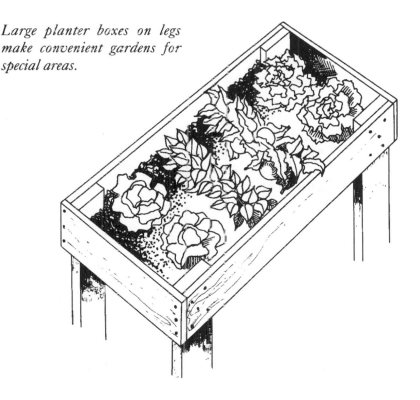

Large planter boxes on legs make convenient gardens for special areas.

don't have access to such soil, buy some from a garden center or nursery. Or, you might have a truckload of fairly good soil delivered that you can gradually build to a higher state of fertility for your concentrated gardening. And, of course, amendments from a well-tended compost heap, supplemented with kitchen refuse, can enrich planter box soil just as much as they do that of other garden plots.

One chore remains before putting the soil in the boxes. Half-inch holes should be drilled in the bottoms for drainage and covered with copper screening. You can provide uniform and gentle watering by setting the hose nozzle deep in a tall glass jar buried in the soil with its top just level with the surface. As water flows up and out of the jar in a gentle stream, it will spread evenly throughout the bed. And don't let water go to waste when it begins to seep through the bottom of the boxes. Set a plant or two below to take up what soaks through.

This type of gardening has many advantages, not the least of which is being eye to eye with any insect pests that decide to invade. Weeds are quickly spotted, too, and just as quickly pulled from the loose, friable soil. And no-stoop harvesting is a real joy!

Your Lawn

With the vegetables placed in borders or raised beds, your lawn will be walked on in much the same way as garden paths. If you don't want bare patches, it must also receive attention.

The lawn grass you choose should be the type that grows best and most vigorously in your soil and geographical area. In Chapter 7 there is a listing of lawn grasses and the soil pH in which each grows best. A soil test (or a survey of several neighboring lawns) can give you more information if you are undecided.

To Fence or Not To Fence

A fence protects property in two ways. Unwanted animals and people are kept out and one's own children and pets are kept in. Of course, not all intruders can be excluded, but a fence acts as a definite deterrent to the casual trespasser (for example, children playing ball in an adjacent yard won't overrun your lawn and flowerbeds).

Cooperative fencing often is seen today, with several congenial neighbors planning their gardens or yards together so that a feeling of open space is maintained. Low wire fences (with posts painted deep green or black to blend in with the shrubbery) may be used to separate lots if children or pets need to be kept in the home yard.

Fences for Wind Deflection. The logical place for a terrace or patio usually is alongside the house unless the prevailing winds are on that side. The best solution is a baffle or louvered fence, or even a solid one with a few holes to permit air passage. You can curve the fence, angle it, or step it up or down to fit the contours of the location. Just be sure to make it high enough to do the job for which it is intended.

Fences can also be temporary to give young, relatively inexpensive plants protection while they grow into thick, tall windbreaks.

If some of your raised garden beds are placed at the front or sides of the house, they may need to be sheltered by a fence. A more inexpensive way to handle this than by installation of full property line fencing is to drive a sturdy stake at the four corners of each bed and run lightweight chicken wire around. When weeding or harvesting is in order, simply remove the wire temporarily and replace it afterwards. Although this entails extra work, it is an easy solution to the problem and certainly is better than having the beds trampled by children or stray animals.

Have a Cold Frame

Intensive gardening yield can benefit greatly from the use of a cold frame. Our own homemade (and very practical) model is simply constructed from a used aluminum screen door and frame (which makes for easy opening and closing), covered with heavy clear plastic, and mounted on cement blocks. It is located and sloped to receive a southern exposure, and we keep it in use almost all year long.

In early spring I start broccoli, cabbage, and buttercrunch lettuce plants in the cold frame. If I use a mixture of soil and sand to retain heat, I can do this as early as February (later if you live in a northern climate). The plants seem to enjoy the fairly cool conditions and grow much larger than they would in a greenhouse.

If I make several short rows of each plant, there still is a bit of room left over to start tomato plants later in the spring. I can add a few peppers or eggplants to my list after transferring the earlier plants to the garden. My broccoli, cabbage, and lettuce plants are strong and sturdy, well able to stand a bit of cool weather outdoors. From these I get my "first taste of green" and enjoy them while making later plantings of the same vegetables directly into the garden.

A cold frame can help to support even the smallest gardens.

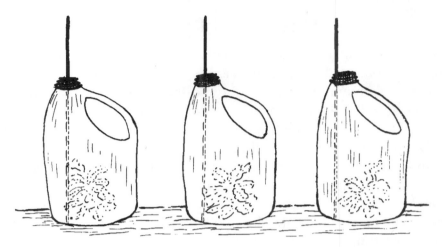

Cut bottoms from plastic jugs to use as hotcaps on transplants and on cold days. Stakes through the tops prevent them from blowing away.

Our early summers in southern Oklahoma are too warm to start more plants of cauliflower, broccoli, Brussels sprouts, cabbage, and lettuce for transplanting into the garden in August, but in a cooler area late spring is a good time. I usually wait for the cool days of early fall to plant them directly outdoors, or I start them in late August in an area of filtered sunlight in my small plastic greenhouse.

In September or October, I plant lettuce in my cold frame again, saving a little space for parsley and other favorite herbs. During mild winters, and by covering the frame on very cold nights, I can have lettuce all winter long.

CHAPTER 3

Small-Garden Techniques

The small garden, particularly in areas where the growing season is short, must take advantage of every growing day. At the same time, it is absolutely necessary to use every possible space-saving technique.

One of the best space-savers is the intercropping of two or more different vegetables in the same piece of ground. Gardeners with plenty of room can leave large spaces between their rows of bush beans, peas, or limas. Such spaces are convenient because they permit the gardener to walk up and down the rows for cultivation or harvesting. However, the small garden can't afford such liberal spacing.

Instead of leaving empty spaces between the pea and bean rows, the intensive gardener should intercrop with lettuce, spinach, and radishes, and with brassicas such as cabbage, cauliflower, broccoli, Brussels sprouts, kale, or collards.

Naturally, the garden is going to look a bit crowded at first, but it will look progressively better once the early peas and quick-maturing lettuce, spinach, and radishes have been harvested, and the pea vines and lettuce stumps have been removed and placed in the compost bin. By that time, the slower-growing brassicas will be spreading out and using the extra space they will now have.

As summer advances and the early cabbage and cauliflower begin to mature and are harvested, set your early tomato plants out right next to the heading cabbages. Again, the brassicas will be harvested out of the way in time for the tomatoes to fill the space. With intercropping, you don't wait for the first crop to be out before putting in another one; you keep plants moving out and in all during the growing season.

Another time-honored intercropping practice is to plant vining squash next to corn (if you've arranged room for it): This smothers weed seedlings and keeps the soil around the corn hills moist. Plant your squash seed after the corn is out of the ground so they will have a head start and not be smothered by the quick-growing squash. If you practice this technique, you must take a firm hand with the squash vines, keeping them in bounds and training them to go where you want them. Work from both sides of the narrow beds.

Another good vegetable to plant with corn, especially in the southern United States, is black-eyed peas. These, too, should be planted just after the corn is out of the ground. Black-eyed peas climb up the corn stalks to seek light but are not detrimental to the corn. After the corn ears have been harvested, the still-standing stalks will soon be completely covered with the vines. I've grown an enormous crops of both corn and black-eyed peas using this method.

Catch Cropping

This space-saving method is a little different from intercropping: You plan to grow a quick-to-mature vegetable in ground you've reserved for a later planting of a slower-growing vegetable. How you use this technique depends on what you plan to grow. Here is how I do it: Our garden is prepared for planting in early spring, but my young plants of cabbage, broccoli, and Brussels sprouts usually are not yet ready for setting out. I don't want the garden to be idle, so I sow radishes, lettuce (with emphasis on leaf types), and spinach to get a quick crop before setting out the brassicas.

If I grow a heading-type lettuce, I sometimes later remove every other plant when I set in the broccoli. By the time the lettuce has been harvested, the cabbage or broccoli can have all the room. And when I set out any of the brassicas I also take precautions against cutworms: Collar the plants with cardboard set 2 inches below the soil and 1 inch above, or place a nail or small stick immediately beside the plant stem so the cutworm cannot wrap itself around the stem and cut it off.

Succession Cropping

Succession cropping is not actually a space-saver, but rather, a way to increase the total yield from your garden each season, which is one of our principal objectives.

Succession cropping keeps the garden soil in action for crop production rather than leaving any part of it unused at any time. As soon as one crop is out of the ground, the soil is quickly prepared to receive another. Depending on the section of the country in which you live, this technique can be used two, three, or more times each growing season.

After the early spring, cool-weather crops have been harvested, you can begin to sow bush beans (green or yellow, or both) and bush limas. You also should fill in the empty places where your early potatoes have been dug. Now is a good time to plant salad onions and more radishes, lettuce, or bush beans.

Succession cropping is much like catch cropping, but with one important difference: With catch cropping, quick-to-grow vegetables are grown *before* the same ground is wanted for a main-crop vegetable; with succession cropping, any crop, whether it be quick- or slow-growing, is sown or planted in ground from which another crop has just been harvested. Here are some winning succession combinations that have given me good results over the years I have been gardening.

We like peas so much that we plan for a continuous harvest. All pea varieties are planted on the same day, but they ripen progressively at their appointed time, according to variety. To make the most of our space, I plant peas in double rows and give them a fence or trellis to climb on. When the peas are finished bearing in late spring, I remove the fence and pull up any weeds (as well as the vines) and place them in the compost bin.

To prepare the soil for our second crop, I loosen the soil where the double row of peas were located, but leave the mulch undisturbed. Turnips and rutabagas are then seeded in the rows rather thickly, for the tops are delicious when young and make excellent greens. Thinning gives the remaining plants more room to develop.

Some years, if I do not want to plant turnips until early fall, I leave the fence and mulch that remains, and loosen the soil for a crop of climbing beans such as scarlet runner or Kentucky Wonder. This works especially well if you live in a southern area because beans like hot weather.

Kohlrabi and beets are two of our favorite vegetables (and they are also believed to benefit each other when grown together). Kohlrabi is best when crisp and young, so I pull it early and follow it with a late crop of beets.

Onions of all types stand cold well — in fact, I grow Egyptian or "tree" onions and shallots all winter long. For table onions, I buy bunches of young green onions and plant them in early spring, so they are one of the first vegetables to go into the garden. I make triple rows of onions and plant them just 2 or 3 inches apart but stagger the two outer rows so that the onions grow between the ones in the middle row. If you want to leave some of these for mature onions, thin them alternately as they grow and leave space for those left to grow larger. If all of them are to be used for young green salad onions, you can begin planting peanuts or black-eyed peas between the onions in late spring when the ground is sufficiently warm.

There are other efficient combinations: Early carrots may be followed by kale, early beets by fall lettuce. Radishes, which discourage the striped cucumber beetle, may be followed by melons or cucumbers. As a protective measure, leave a few radishes to grow (and even go to seed) when you plant your melons later in the spring.

There are many combinations for succession planting that can be worked out successfully by the individual gardener according to likes and dislikes, but there are a few rules to remember. For example, root crops use up potash, so you will have better results if you replace carrots or beets with a leafy top vegetable, such as lettuce or spinach, rather than with another root crop. On the other hand, leafy crops need a lot of nitrogen and thus should not succeed each other. Late cabbage or lettuce succeeding peas thrive on the nitrogen that the peas have added to the soil. Corn, which also needs nitrogen to grow well, also does well planted after peas.

The trick in succession planting is to leave no idle ground. When a plant is through growing, pull it out at once and sow the seed of another crop in its place, or transplant a seedling from your cold frame or nursery row.

Opposite: A 6 x 10-foot minigarden shows the first planting at top left, succession crops at top right, summer planting at bottom left and early fall crops at bottom right.

EARLY SPRING

FOLLOWED BY FALL PEAS	LATE PEAS
EARLY PEAS	
BEETS	SWISS CHARD
CARROTS	CHIVES
ONIONS	CABBAGE
LETTUCE	RADISHES
SPINACH	BROCCOLI

BRICK WALK

LATE SPRING

FOLLOWED BY POLE BEANS	FOLLOWED BY POLE BEANS
KOHLRABI	PARSNIPS
BUSH BEANS GREENS	CAULIFLOWER
SPINACH	PARSLEY
EARLY TOMATOES	BUSH BEANS WAX
MID SEASON TOMATOES	BUSH SQUASH

BRICK WALK

SUMMER

FOLLOWED BY LIMA BEANS	CELERY PLANTS
FOLLOWED BY FALL PEAS	
ZUCCHINI	EGGPLANT
MELONS	TAMPALA
RHUBARB CHARD	SQUASH
LATE TOMATOES	CUCUMBERS
PEPPERS	

BRICK WALK

FALL

FOLLOWED BY CAULIFLOWER	FOLLOWED BY WINTER SQUASH
CARROTS	LATE CABBAGE
BRUSSEL SPROUTS	COLLARDS
KALE	WINTER ONIONS
CELERY CABBAGE	TURNIPS
ONIONS	LEEKS

Feed Your Soil

Succession crops are ideal for the intensive garden but you must feed your soil as you go along or it will quickly become depleted. As an organic gardener I think that this feeding should be of composted organic materials, which not only supply nutrients in usable form but also improve the texture of the soil itself. Root crops, in particular, grow better and gain taste and crisp succulence in loose, friable soil. Compost may be dug directly into the soil or used as a side dressing. Mulches of leaves, hay, lawn clippings, or other organic materials are useful to conserve moisture and add nutrients as they break down and decompose.

Even if you have only a bucketful of compost at a time to put on some part of your planting, it is worth adding it. Try to keep a season-long, steady supply of nutrients going into the soil for a good, continuous harvest. Succession planting keeps you going along steadily, too. Is it worth it? You bet!

Vertical Gardening

Don't allow your vining plants to sprawl: It wastes valuable space, lets pests get at them, and taxes your aching back at harvest time. Vertical gardening pushes the plant growth upward, which makes additional production possible in a small space.

A friend of mine had a tiny, squarish space behind her garage. She erected what might be called a vine tepee or wigwam, using four tall poles fastened together near the top with soft wire tied from pole to pole. One year she planted pole beans, which climb vigorously. When they reached the top, they simply rambled downward again after a brief period of waving their tendrils in the air. Soon the whole wigwam was covered with a mass of productive vines. The easy-to-harvest beans could be picked by the handfuls. Scarlet runner beans, which climb rapidly and give a wonderful display of bright flowers, are particularly attractive when grown like this.

Another spring, she decided to try vining squash. This proved to be a good choice as well but required a bit more attention. Unlike pole beans, which climb without assistance, squash plants need to be tied loosely here and there to the poles. When the vines reached the top of the poles, she stopped them by pinching out the growing point at the top of each plant, causing the plants to produce lots of side shoots.

Squash trained upward on a pole teepee receive more sun and take less room.

Discarded lampshade frames make good supports for small, bushy plants.

The side-shoot tendrils grasped the twine wound from pole to pole of the tepee. Before long the whole structure was covered with green leaves and attractive yellow flowers, which eventually produced a quantity of delicious squash.

Tomato towers are another solution worthy of mention. They are made from circles of concrete-reinforcing wire, which is sturdy, strong, and has a wide mesh that makes harvesting easy. The plants are enclosed within each circle, and because their growth is forced upward, they climb to amazing heights. The fruit have the advantage of plenty of sunshine, are easy to see, and can be harvested standing up. And of course the "towers" are reusable almost indefinitely if stored carefully in the fall. If you live in an especially windy area, drive a stake down on one side of the wire enclosure.

Towers are useful for other things besides tomatoes — they can accommodate several cucumber, squash, or melon plants. Many kinds of peas and beans (including limas) can be successfully grown in them. Just for fun, you might like to place one in a flowerbed and grow several different types of ornamental gourds. Pole beans and morning glories do amazingly well together in a tower. In fact, if you are really pressed for space, grow several different vining vegetables together. They are quite compatible.

Two-Level Gardening

I didn't invent this gardening system, but I practice it and talk about it so much that one might think I were trying to take the credit. As a space-saver and a way to get more variety in small garden areas, I think it is one of the very best.

Vegetables that occupy different *levels* of the soil often make excellent companions in the garden row. Because one vegetable grows and fruits above the soil and the other below, they can be planted more closely together than is usual.

Good two-level combinations are the various members of the onion family grown below the ground, and lettuce, tomatoes, and even strawberries grown above it. Garlic, the strong member, also protects tomatoes against both the red spider and the tomato worm.

Other good combinations to plant are leeks with vining plants, carrots with peas, and beets with kohlrabi. The many possibilities are limited only by your imagination. Plant these vegetables together in the

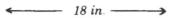

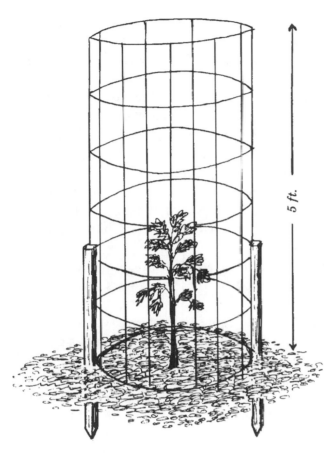

18 in.

5 ft.

Vine towers made from concrete-reinforcing wire are fine for tall plants like tomatoes.

same row and space them just a few inches apart, according to variety.

Also, when I am growing wide-spreading plants like broccoli, Brussels sprouts, cauliflower, or Chinese celery cabbage, I never let the spaces between them go to waste. While I'm waiting for them to mature, I add a crop or two of radishes or some other quick-growing vegetable in between the plants. You might call this two-level catch cropping!

However, you must be careful when two-leveling not to plant together those plants that compete for the same space and light — such as pole beans and sunflowers. Also, don't juxtapose plants that react unfavorably to each other, such as carrots and dill, or onions and peas or beans. (See my book, *Carrots Love Tomatoes,* listed in the Appendix under *Other Books From Storey Communications You'll Enjoy.*)

Terrace Gardening

Very clever those Chinese — and very big on conservation! It is important to them (as it should be to us) for two reasons. First, it is necessary because everything possible must be meticulously saved to make a living, and second, it is part of the deep feeling of the Chinese that one particular piece of land is *home* to a family. Are we any different?

The soil, which is so vital to the Chinese, has been carefully saved through hundreds of years of cultivation, and one of their most important means of conserving it has been and is by terracing, which allows farming of the steep sides of China's hills.

What has this to do with you? Nothing, if your lot is level; but, if your home is perched on sloping ground and you want a garden that won't wash away, it may be worthwhile to take a leaf from the Chinese farmer's notebook.

Through the centuries they have terraced their slopes — leveled the land like huge stairsteps. Crops grow on these level areas and rain does not wash the soil away.

With old railroad ties, bricks, stone, or cement blocks you can do the same thing on a smaller scale, even making a steep hillside into a garden. If your area is large enough, a tiller will help you with the initial preparations. The width of each terrace depends on the degree of the slope. Keep making passes across the slope with the tiller (always working from top to bottom of the slope) until about a foot of tilled soil rises above the untilled earth. Then, provide for another 2-foot width of path before starting another terrace at the next lower level.

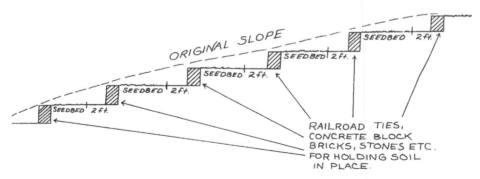

A southerly slope can be terraced effectively for plant beds with a tiller.

Narrow terrace steps (or staggered containers) allow more plants to thrive in a small space and also allow each one adequate sunlight.

By treating each terrace as a separate garden, it is even possible to tailor each soil level organically for specific crops, keeping in mind the needed acidity or alkalinity, richness, and texture. For example, you can plan your strawberry bed level with rather acid, coarse materials, such as tilled-in leaves, and expect good results. However, the soil texture would need to be much finer for small seeds such as lettuce.

Space should be allowed for lateral paths to divide the terraces conveniently. This permits you to walk "across" your garden without stepping on plowed or planted soil sections. You also can do your weed-pulling and thinning while standing in the paths below. In time, the paths will become packed, forming shallow waterways to carry off excessive rain. If the paths are seeded or sodded to grass, this will act as an added erosion-reducing safeguard.

When your terraces are settled and firm, begin digging under quantities of leaves. In addition to improving the soil, they will soak up a lot of moisture and prevent leaching and erosion. Autumn is the best time to dig leaves under in preparation for spring planting. Just as with other gardens, you may dig in vegetable residues and other clean garbage from time to time.

So, even if your backyard slopes, you don't have to give up gardening. Terracing gives you good garden control even when conditions are difficult. In fact, if your backyard has a good southern exposure (as it should), and you live well north, you will gain more weeks of growing time with terraced beds than from level ones.

Tier Gardening

People have been using built-up pyramids, or tiers, for a long time to grow a lot of plants in a small space. And tiers work very well, particularly with strawberries, for instance, when equipped with a central sprinkling system (which usually comes with the kit). Unlike terrace gardening, the tier garden usually is placed on level land and is just as useful when planted for vegetables as it is for fruit.

A well-kept tier garden is attractive anywhere and might even be made a feature of your front yard, although you might wish to combine vegetables and flowers for a more decorative effect. And, it doesn't have to be round, as most of the strawberry pyramids are. In a cool climate, you will find the soil in your pyramid warms up faster, permitting earlier planting and thus lengthening your growing season.

The Garden Fence

No discussion of vertical gardening would be complete without suggestions for using every bit of the property fencing. Growing big pumpkins would not be practical, but I have grown *Small Sugar* several times. Like squash, it is a rambler, but climbs upward with a bit of coaxing — sometimes even without it. So, if your family is fond of pumpkin pie, you *can* grow your own. A few vines produce extravagantly, and because frozen pumpkin keeps well, I grow them about every third year.

Of course, cucumbers, beans, and peas of all types will grow on a fence. Berry vines, too, may be tied to a fence for support and convenience and, if the fence is sufficiently strong and permits good air circulation, a few grape vines (possibly spaced with morning glories, climbing nasturtiums, or climbing roses) will give you both beauty and the luxury of fresh fruit. From my point of view, a property fence is very worthwhile, both for protection and privacy and for the added space it provides for growing vegetables, fruit, and flowers.

You may even want some additional "fences" in the garden areas. Try growing climbing vegetables on nylon nets along the back of the garden beds. Pepper plants grown in good fertile soil are apt to be quite

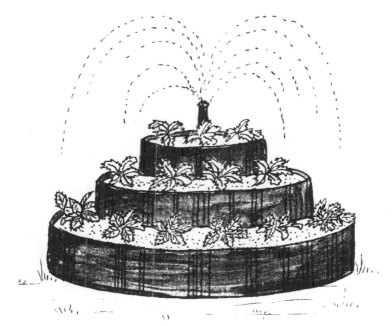

A strawberry pyramid, both decorative and efficient, may be used for other crops, too.

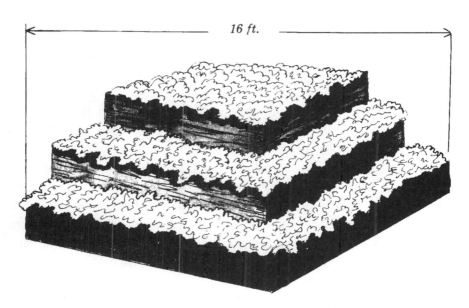

16 ft.

Pyramid garden of stacked railroad ties saves space and bending over.

A wire A-frame with removable sheet plastic cover helps tender plants in spring and on cold nights.

brittle (a quality also reflected in the crispness and succulence of the fruit), but if they are staked or tied to a fence or put in a wire enclosure, the branches will not be broken by high winds or by being brushed against.

Edible Flowering Screens. Fences, permanent or temporary, may serve as screens. The height depends on the feature or object you wish to make less noticeable. Such a screen also often provides a windbreak, gives shade and privacy to a small yard, or conceals a small building. And, it makes sense to grow something both edible and attractive.

The scarlet runner bean, which is both edible and beautiful, comes to mind first for this purpose. Another possibility, the hyacinth bean, has lovely, mild-scented blossoms on its vine and is a rampant grower with highly decorative large, smooth, bright green leaves. As the blossoms complete their flowering cycle, green pods are formed, each containing several pea-like seeds that taste much like fresh garden peas when cooked and seasoned. The flowers may be purple or white.

I think that climbing cucumbers of the Japanese type are especially pretty with their attractive yellow flowers and long, slender fruits, as are gourds, many of which are edible when young. The Luffa sponge gourds are beloved of Oriental cooks, who stuff the young fruits and bake them like squash. When the gourd is fully mature, you can peel off the hard skin and find inside a durable fibrous sponge that is useful for kitchen or bath, or to wash the car!

You might even want to try climbing spinach. This unusual, quick-growing vine produces a lot of tasty bright greens, and because they are ready to use by midsummer, they make an excellent hot-weather substitute for regular spinach.

If your screen is in a sufficiently sunny spot, consider the climbing tomatoes. All tomatoes may be trained upward, but I am speaking of the true climbers. Give them a little assistance to start by tying here and there, and they can grow as high as 10 to 18 feet while producing large, well-flavored red tomatoes often weighing over a pound each.

Among the climbing fruits is the hardy *Beta* grape, which grows well even in the northern United States. It is a fast-growing vine that also produces big crops of tangy blue grapes good for jam and jelly. The vegetable pear or mirliton, a little-known vine that produces exceedingly well in the southern United States, is beautiful, fast-growing, and yields light-green fruits that are simply delicious. So, if you want to hide your garbage cans or compost bin, don't hesitate — plant an edible, flowering screen.

Rent a Garden

I have one final suggestion for those who would like to garden but have absolutely no space at all. Apartment dwellers, too, get the urge to garden come spring, and they *can* have something more than a window box for plants.

A small grape arbor of just two vines can be practical and beautiful.

Why not place a want-ad in your local paper to rent some garden land? Simply explain why and how you want to use the lot or land: You may be surprised at the replies you receive. You may even have several choices.

If possible, choose land that has previously been under cultivation. Sometimes, for reasons such as the owner's age, infirmity, or lack of time, a former garden plot is going unused. You may even be able to use it free if you agree to share some of the produce with the owner.

Another possibility is a city lot that the owner will permit you to use just for keeping down the weeds. For several years I worked a lot like this and used it for the "space hogs" I did not have room for in our small backyard garden. I grew several rows of corn, and over part of it rambled vining squash, cucumbers, and pumpkins. The land was reasonably fertile and everything grew well. When the lot came up for sale a few years later, I was given the first option to buy it and did: Luckily, it adjoined my property to the south. In time, I fenced it, continued to build up the soil, and have enjoyed its use ever since.

In scattered municipalities across the country, community garden plots, usually organized under civic auspices, are available for annual rental. Quite often, rental includes spring tilling of the plot, and sometimes public transportation to the garden areas is provided as well. For more information write to the American Community Gardening Association, 325 Walnut Street, Philadelphia, PA 19106.

However, if you do decide to rent a garden, there are several factors you should consider. One of the most important is the availability of water. You'll also need to transport your tools from your home, and the possibility of vandalism must be considered today. On an open, unfenced lot, this may prove to be a problem, and general protection is usually lacking in these arrangements. Consider any plots offered from these viewpoints and try to make a wise choice.

CHAPTER 4

Which Vegetables and Herbs Will You Grow?

Which vegetables are best for the small garden — the standard or the midget varieties? The obvious choice is the smaller ones that take up the least space and make it possible to grow more in a small area. But, suppose you and your family happen to like corn, squash, and tall-growing okra? Can these vegetables find happiness in the minigarden? Yes, I think they can, but because not everything will fit in a small space, you'll have to make choices.

One aid is a special box for vining squash that is placed so the squash does not smother other vegetables by growing over them. Pumpkins and even sweet potatoes could be treated the same way. And, by careful choice of both standard and midget varieties, it is possible to have just about any vegetable you want to grow, even in a small space.

Standard-Sized Vegetables

Beets, carrots, leaf lettuce, onions, early peas, radishes, and spinach can be planted in rows 1 foot apart, provided your soil has been brought to a high state of fertility. Other vegetables need more room. Tomato plants should be at least 2 feet apart in rows 3 feet apart (if you have more than one row).

Sweet corn usually is planted in hills 3 feet apart each way or in rows 2½ feet apart with each plant 1 foot apart. Actually, corn may be planted much closer if a good mulching program is followed. If you eliminate paths between the rows, you can space your rows and the plants in the rows 1 foot apart.

You can plant your corn even closer by reducing the distance between rows by 1 inch and planting each kernel of corn in each row opposite the gap between each pair in the next row. By staggering the kernels this way, you actually increase the distance from every plant in each row to the nearest plant in the row beside it, and with this method you could even make your rows 10 inches apart.

If other factors such as high fertility and plenty of sunlight are equal, you will still have a crop, and in a small garden every inch saved counts. Corn, which is wind-pollinated, is a perfect candidate for raised beds, with each variety planted in a solid block. Remember that to harvest the ears from plants growing so close together, your beds must be narrow enough for you to reach from one or both sides.

Cucumbers, melons, and squash require a good 2½ to 5 feet of space in all directions. But cucumbers can be grown on a fence to save space, and the fence does not have to be *around* your garden or property line.

Last year, I put a short length of fence right in the garden, secured it with iron stakes, and grew our cucumbers on it. I cultivated on both sides, mulching heavily to conserve moisture as the season advanced. A further bonus of this method was the straightness of the cucumbers. I

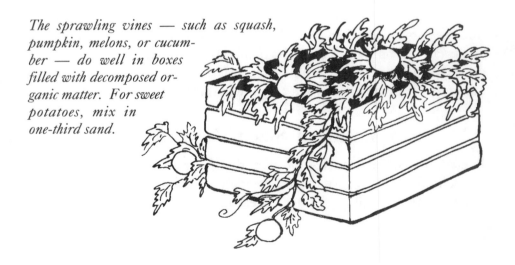

The sprawling vines — such as squash, pumpkin, melons, or cucumber — do well in boxes filled with decomposed organic matter. For sweet potatoes, mix in one-third sand.

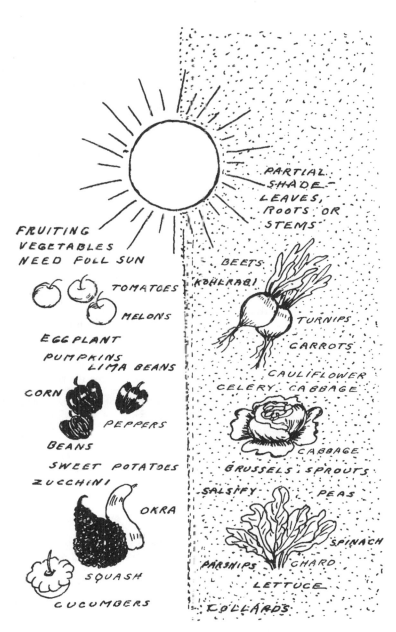

FRUITING
VEGETABLES
NEED FULL SUN

TOMATOES

MELONS

EGGPLANT

PUMPKINS

LIMA BEANS

CORN

PEPPERS

BEANS

SWEET POTATOES

ZUCCHINI

OKRA

SQUASH

CUCUMBERS

PARTIAL
SHADE—
LEAVES,
ROOTS OR
STEMS

BEETS

KOHLRABI

TURNIPS

CARROTS

CAULIFLOWER

CELERY CABBAGE

CABBAGE

BRUSSELS SPROUTS

SALSIFY

PEAS

SPINACH

PARSNIPS

CHARD

LETTUCE

COLLARDS

Sunlight and shade needs vary for different vegetables.

Capsule Guide to Garden Problems

Symptoms	Probable Cause	Possible Cures
Dying young plants	Fertilizer burn	Mix fertilizer thoroughly with soil.
	Disease (damping off)	Treat seed; don't over-water.
Stunted plants, pale green to yellow	Low soil fertility	Test soil for fertilizer recommendation.
	Low soil pH (too acid)	Test soil for amount of lime needed.
	Poor soil drainage	Add organic matter.
	Shallow or compacted soil	Plow deeper.
	Insects or diseases	Identify and use control measures.
	Nematodes	Test soil for treatment recommendations.
Stunted plants, purplish color	Low temperature	Plant at recommended time; use row cover to increase temperature.
	Lack of phosphorus	Add phosphorus fertilizer.
Holes in leaves	Insects	Identify and use control measures.
	Hail	Be thankful it was not worse!
Spots, molds, darkened areas in leaves and stems	Disease	Identify, spray, or dust (use resistant varieties).
	Chemical burn	Use treatment at recommended rate.
	Fertilizer burn	Keep fertilizer off plants.
Wilting plants	Dry soil	Irrigate if possible.
	Excess water in soil	Drain.
	Nematodes	Test soil for treatment recommendations.

Capsule Guide to Garden Problems (cont'd)

Symptoms	Probable Cause	Possible Cures
Weak, spindly plants	Too much shade	Remove shade or move plants to sunny spot.
	Too much water	Reduce watering.
	Plants too thick	Seed at recommended rate.
	Too much nitrogen	Avoid excess fertilization.
Failure to set fruit	High temperature	Follow recommended planting time.
	Low temperature	Follow recommended planting time.
	Too much nitrogen	Avoid excess fertilization.
	Insects	Identify and use control measures.
Tomato leaf curl	Heavy pruning in hot weather	Don't prune.
	Disease	Identify and use control measures.
Dry brown or black rot on blossom end of tomato	Low soil calcium	Add liming material.
	Extremely dry soil	Irrigate.
Misshapen tomatoes (catfacing)	Cool weather during blooming	Plant at recommended time.
Abnormal leaves and growth	Viral disease	Remove and dispose of infected plants to prevent spreading. Control insects that transmit.

(Courtesy of Stokes Seed Company)

like the long, crispy, small-seeded Burpee *Burpless,* which tends to curl a bit if the vines are allowed to sprawl on the ground. Their shape is greatly improved if grown on a fence or trellis.

Most types of melons do take a lot of room, but as with squash, much space can be saved by growing bush varieties. Of course, all of these spacings are intended for hand cultivation. If you intend to use a tiller or cultivator, you need to allow for a lot more room between rows.

If your garden area has a considerable slope (preferably to the south), make the rows across the grade to help check erosion during heavy rains. And remember to plant tall-growing vegetables at the north or west side of your plot to prevent them from shading shorter-growing varieties.

Sunlight and Shade

These are both important garden factors, and gardeners on small plots have to consider them very carefully. With this in mind, I've included a *Vegetable Planting Guide* (see Appendix) for many of the most widely planted garden vegetables. Even if your available garden space has a lot of shade, you can still grow many vegetables that do not require full sunlight. Save your sunny spots for those that do — such as cucumbers, eggplant, peppers, squash, corn, and tomatoes.

What Will Fit

If your garden is to be really tiny (about 4 by 8 feet), plan on planting a half row each of radishes and leaf lettuce (to be followed by a succession planting of snap beans), a row of snap beans planted at the regular time, and a few tomato plants.

With a little more space (about 250 square feet) you can plant snap beans, lima beans, beets, broccoli, carrots, cabbage, a hill or two of cucumbers, greens (such as spinach, Swiss chard, amaranth, leaf and head lettuce), as well as a row of early peas. And you can fit in a half-dozen tomato plants, too.

With plenty of room (well over 250 square feet) you can also include Brussels sprouts, cauliflower, sweet corn, eggplant, melons, onions, two or more rows of peas, peppers, squash, and any other vegetables of which you are especially fond.

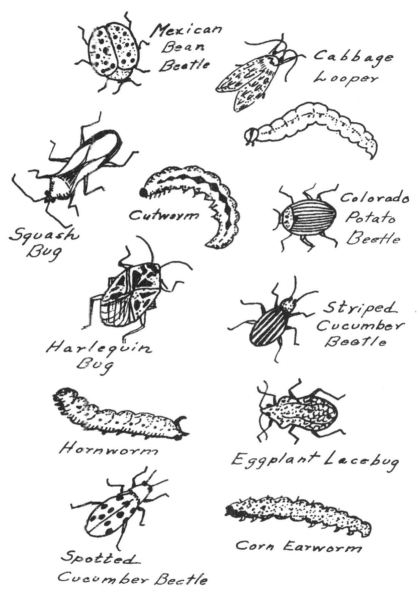

Mexican Bean Beetle

Cabbage Looper

Squash Bug

Cutworm

Colorado Potato Beetle

Harlequin Bug

Striped Cucumber Beetle

Hornworm

Eggplant Lacebug

Spotted Cucumber Beetle

Corn Earworm

Recognition of harmful insects is half the battle. Check for them daily.

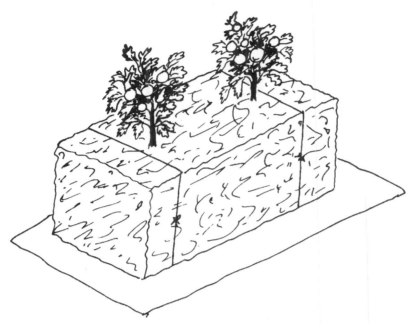

A way to plant tomatoes anywhere: Soak a bale of alfalfa hay well with water for 3 to 6 weeks, then punch two deep holes in the bale top and place a plant in each. Keep in full sun and well watered.

Choosing Regular-Sized Varieties

With all the seed catalog pictures of vegetables at their peak of perfection and in glowing colors, the choices are difficult and bewildering, especially for the new gardener. To make things even more confusing, some of the vegetables do not do well in the northern (or southern) United States because of climate. Some vegetables, such as okra, need a warm climate, whereas others like parsnips and rutabagas need a long, fairly cool growing season (in the southern United States they often become woody and tough).

You can secure from your County Extension Agent the names of varieties best suited to your area, and you can consult with gardening neighbors who have found out by trial and error which crops grow best. You probably want to do a little experimenting from year to year, too, as new varieties are introduced.

Open-Pollinated Varieties or Hybrids?

The seed from open-pollinated varieties produces new plants very similar to those of the mother plant. Nature takes care of the pollination, and all we need to do is save the seed from year to year and plant it. Many of these varieties are older heirloom vegetables that have been passed down from generation to generation. They include some of the tastiest varieties — especially some of the old-time tomatoes. So, keep saving and sharing seed from these open-pollinated treasures. They are a part of our plant heritage, and we must not let them disappear.

Hybrids, on the other hand, are produced by carefully controlled cross-pollination and do not grow true from seed. They are developed for many reasons, such as disease resistance and compact growth habit, and often are more vigorous than the open-pollinated varieties. Some are bred for commercial production, where uniform ripening, ease of shipping, and cosmetic appearance are important. I recommend many hybrid varieties, but be sure to choose ones that are bred for smaller growers, like home gardeners, where taste is more important than appearance.

I've grown *Big Boy* for years and still grow it, although *Better Boy* is even more productive in my garden: Both varieties are so good I don't want to give up either one! I find hybrid cucumbers to be extremely disease-resistant, and they bear heavily all summer long. Hybrid squash, even though it starts bearing early, continues vigorously until the end of the growing season.

I consider hybrid sweet corn a "must." By choosing the right varieties, I can plant them all at the same time in the spring but have them ripen successively for over a month. In this way, I can sow them when soil and weather conditions are most favorable and time the planting to avoid the worst infestation of corn borers. (And remember, hybrid corn should never be planted in one long row. To ensure pollination and development of plump ears, plant *each variety* in a block of short rows.) Hybrid eggplant and melons grow exceptionally well, too, and I find hybrid onions grow larger and are more succulent.

However, to have your hybrid vegetables do well, it is absolutely necessary to maintain a high level of soil fertility and give them plenty of water. These varieties are such strong growers and produce such large crops that they must have plenty of food and water throughout the growing season.

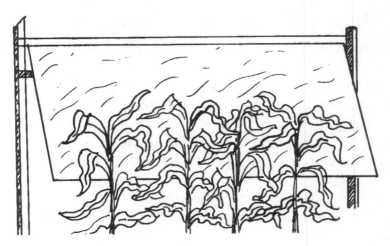

When a planting such as corn is getting too much shade, a reflective panel of aluminum or a white board helps the growth.

Those Fascinating Midgets

Midget, as applied to garden vegetables, is an all-encompassing word, but you have to be careful how you use it. There actually are three types of midget vegetables.

One type is the dwarf plant that produces normal-sized fruit, such as bush squash and some types of bush cucumbers. The second type is the normal-sized plant that produces diminutive fruit, such as the small-fruited squash, *Table Queen*. The third type is the diminutive plant that produces diminutive fruit, such as *Tiny Tim* tomato. For the home gardener who must make the most of a small space, this third category usually is the most popular, but consider the first type, too.

Tom Thumb lettuce can be planted in rows no more than 6 inches apart with plants 4- to 6-inches apart in the row. If the rows are this close together, it is good to stagger the plants. *Tiny Tim* tomato occupies a space more or less circular, with a diameter of 18 to 24 inches and a height of 12 to 18 inches. Honeybush muskmelon produces 5- to 7-inch cantaloupes, just right for individual servings, and they ripen in only 82 days. The small vines can be counted on to produce three to six luscious little melons with a high sugar content. *Goldcrop* wax bush bean is very resistant to virus diseases and produces a heavy crop of fine quality 5- to 6-inch pods.

Little Finger miniature carrot can be pulled early. *Pixie Hybrid* tomato, specifically designed for growing in pots, window boxes, or in flower borders, grows 14- to 18-inches tall and bears heavy loads of bright scarlet fruits about 1¾ inches in diameter.

Golden Nugget is an extremely prolific bush squash well suited for the small garden. The compact bushes bear from three to six fruits of 1½ to 2 pounds, just the right size for baking in the shell. The fruit is bright orange, the flesh deep yellow, and the taste and quality compare favorably to those of *Buttercup. Early Salad Hybrid* tomato grows only 6- to 8-inches high, with a spread of a little more than 2 feet. Each plant produces 250 to 300 delicious fruit that remain on the plant in good condition for a full month, even in hot weather. This tomato not only

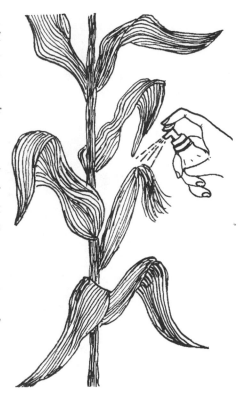

Spray mineral oil on young corn silks to foil corn earworms.

bears early but continues to produce a seemingly endless crop for 2 months or more, or until killed by frost. And the quality is simply great.

If you like midget watermelons, there are a lot of reasons for growing them. For one thing, these watermelons, such as *Sugar Baby*, seem less finicky about weather conditions, and produce even when conditions are not perfect (when large melons are thrown off course). Their convenient size of about 8 inches in diameter is another advantage, for most will fit easily into refrigerators without cutting.

To succeed with midget watermelons, follow a few simple rules: Start them indoors in peat pots about 2 weeks before transplanting outdoors, plant in full sun, water regularly, and plant in organically enriched soil.

Here are some more small-sized varieties to look for:

Bean: Romano, Royal Burgundy, Venture

Beet: Detroit Dark Red, Early Wonder, Burpee's Golden, Cylindra, Boltardy

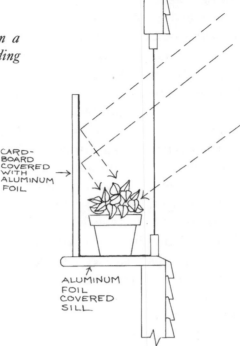

Pots of herbs and other plants on a windowsill gain sun benefit by adding a reflecting backing board.

CARD-BOARD COVERED WITH ALUMINUM FOIL →

↑ ALUMINUM FOIL COVERED SILL

Broccoli: Spartan, Green Comet, Italian Green Sprouting, DiCicco

Brussels Sprout: Jade Cross Hybrid, Long Island Improved

Cabbage: Earliana, Early Jersey Wakefield, Copenhagen Market, Red Ace, Ruby Ball Hybrid, Red Head Hybrid

Carrot: Little Finger, Ox-Heart, Baby Finger, Royal Chantenay, Spartan Bonus, Nantes, Short 'n' Sweet, Gold Pak

Cauliflower: Early Snowball, Snow King Hybrid, Snow Crown Hybrid, Purple Head

Cucumber: Table Queen, Burpee Hybrid, Bush Whopper, Salad Bush, Park's Burpless Bush, Pot Luck, Patio Pik, Burpless Early Pik, Crispy Salty, Tiny Dill Cuke

Eggplant: Slim Jim, Ichiban, Black Beauty, Long Tom, Jersey King Hybrid, Small Ruffled Red, Thai Green

Lettuce: Tom Thumb, Oak Leaf, Buttercrunch, Salad Bowl, Dark Green Boston, Ruby, Bigg, Tendercrunch

Pea: Sugar Snap, Snowbird, Mighty Midget, Alaska, Little Marvel, Frosty, Green Arrow, Dwarf Gray Sugar, Burpee Sweet Pod

Pepper: Bell – Bell Boy, Keystone Resistant, California Wonder, New

Ace, World-beater; Hot Red Cherry, Long Red Cayenne, Jalapeño, Thai Hot

Potato: Chippewa, Duke of York, Early Gem, Red McClure, White Cobbler

Radish: Cherry Belle, Scarlet Globe

Onion: White Sweet Spanish, Yellow Sweet Spanish, Southport Yellow Globe

Spinach: Melody, Long-Standing Bloomsdale, America, Avon Hybrid

Swiss Chard: Fordhook Giant, Burpee's Rhubarb Chard

Tomato: Tiny Tim, Patio, Pixie, Small Fry VFM, Toy Boy, Better Bush, Heartland, Stupice

Watermelon: Sugar Baby

Space permits me to list only a few of the outstanding midget vegetable varieties available. For additional varieties, contact the seed houses listed in the Appendix under *Sources of Supply.*

Herbs for Shady Spots

Any time an herb garden is mentioned, most of us immediately visualize a sunny border, bed, or rockery, but for many herbs this isn't necessary. Here are some herbs you can grow successfully in shade or part shade, and hints on how to do it.

Angelica favors cool, moist shade, well-drained and medium-rich soil; it is a tall plant.

Basil is delicious with tomatoes and grows well in their shade, particularly if the tomatoes are trained to grow upward so they don't sprawl over it.

Bedstraw forms a dense ground cover and likes ample moisture.

Catnip is easy to germinate, and its seed remains viable for 4 to 5 years.

Costmary is very hardy, grows 2 to 3 feet tall, and suffers no ill effects in shade.

Horehound grows in sun or partial shade; it prefers dry, poor soil.

Lemon Balm, a close relative of the mints, does not have their spreading habits, and does well in all soils. Propagation is best by root division.

Lovage needs rich, deep, moist soil and some shade. It grows to a height of 7 feet!

Many herbs, like the mints, do well in partial shade, such as around the bases of trees. Chervil *prefers well-drained, fairly rich soil and shade or partial shade.*

Chimney flue tiles make ideal containers for herbs.

Mints come in a wide range of flavors. They grow well in sun or shade. You may even have to restrain them a little to keep them from crowding out more delicate neighbors. They respond even more eagerly if given a bit of soil high in organic content and watered when the weather is dry.

Pennyroyal does best in moist clay soil and partial shade.

Sweet Cicely wants the same conditions as chervil; it won't stand full, hot sun.

Sweet Woodruff, used mainly as a ground cover, grows a dense, 5-inch tall mat, and likes moisture and shade.

Tarragon needs partial shade, too, but needs rich, warm, and well-drained soil.

For complete information about growing herbs, read *Growing and Using Herbs Successfully* by Betty E. M. Jacobs (see Appendix, under *Other Books from Storey Communications You'll Enjoy*). This excellent book describes in detail how to grow, propagate, and sell many basic herbs for profit.

CHAPTER 5

Ways to Sow and Save

Seeds still are the gardener's greatest bargain, but there's no question about it — their price is going up just like everything else, and hybrid seeds (which I highly recommend) are the most expensive of all. Efficient gardening also involves efficient use of time and money. So, let's explore some ways to get the most for the money you spend.

Sowing and Growing

Plant Loss. First, make your seeds go farther. Back in the old days when seeds cost less, the advice was, "Plant thickly and thin plants," and we got into the habit of sowing with a lavish hand. Half or more of both seed and plants were wasted, and this wasn't really necessary. If you mix small seed with sand or soil, it helps make the seeds go farther.

Grow Your Own Sets. Onion sets and plants have increased greatly in price, but I find by growing my own from seed I can have all the onions I want for about one-tenth of the price. To save space, they even can be placed in flowerbeds or along the walk between flowers. And onion plants are very easy to grow. There are many other plants you may often purchase and then grow for yourself — and with greater choice of varieties for succulence and flavor. Buy the very best seed and start broccoli, cabbage, cauliflower, Brussels sprouts, tomatoes, peppers, eggplant, melons, cucumbers, and many others indoors. Even corn can be started this way indoors or in your cold frame to get a jump on spring in a short-season climate.

Seed Tips

How Many To Buy? A corollary to not planting as thickly (and losing by thinning) is to buy fewer seeds for your gardens. And, even though the intensive techniques I've suggested call for placing seeds and plants much closer together than is common practice, like most people, you probably overbuy on seeds. And when spring planting is finished (and your succession planting, too), all of us usually find ourselves with partial or even full packets of perfectly good seeds. Will they keep and be good next year? I decided to find the answer.

My County Extension Agent, the United States Department of Agriculture, and a good many seed experts responded — but I still have no definite information on the storage life of seeds. Much of the answer depends on how good the seeds were in the first place — how high their germination potential. My experience over the years with the leading companies tells me that when they say seeds are "fresh," I believe them. So, I start from there.

To germinate quickly, seeds need moderate warmth (near a hot air register is a good place). Be sure to keep the soil moist.

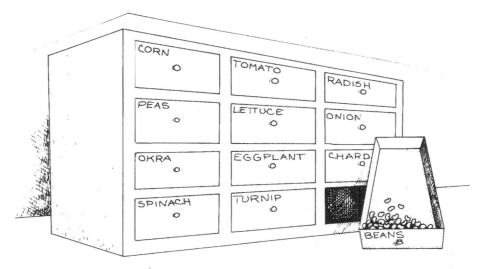

Plastic workbench "organizers" are good for storing seeds. Keep in a dry location.

You can expect the seeds of different vegetable varieties to perform at about the rate shown in the table entitled *Shelf Life of Seeds* that follows and to retain their viability for the numbers of years shown — *provided* they are stored correctly.

Storing Your Seeds. Don't let your leftover seeds lie around. I place them (still in packets) in small, dry, airtight jars (baby food jars are perfect) and put them in the refrigerator. The seeds should be reasonably dry when stored but not bone dry. The ideal temperature is between 36° and 45°F.

Testing Your Seeds. Make a simple germination test before planting, using two shallow dishes. Place a little moist sand in one, and over this spread a piece of flannel that has been sterilized by boiling (or you may use white blotting paper if new sheets are used for each test). The edges of the cloth or paper should be turned down along the sides of the dish so they reach the bottom and act as a wick to draw up the moisture. The sand and cloth or paper should be thoroughly moistened before being placed in the dish.

If blotting paper is used, mark it off into squares with a pencil, and mark the pieces of cloth with pieces of colored cord. Number or label each square and sift onto it a few of the seeds, using only one kind of seed in each division; spread them out evenly. Cover with another dish so that

Shelf Life of Seeds

Vegetable	Average Germination at 1 Year (%)	Average Years of Germination	Number of Seeds Per Ounce
Asparagus	90	3	1,000
Bean, dwarf	90	3	90–100
Beet, garden	80	4	1,750
Cabbage	85	4	5,000
Carrot	75	3	14,000
Cauliflower	75	4	14,000
Corn, sweet	85	3	125
Cucumber	85	5	1,000
Eggplant	75	4	5,000
Lettuce	90	6	12,000–16,000
Muskmelon	85	5	1,200
Mustard	85	3	18,000
Okra	85	1	425
Onion	80	2	12,500
Parsnip	85	1	600
Pea	90	3	50–150
Pepper	75	2	4,000
Pumpkin	90	4	100
Radish	90	4	5,000
Spinach	80	3	3,000
Tomato	85	3	6,000–7,500
Turnip	90	4	10,000
Watermelon	85	5	175–225

air is almost entirely excluded, and place the test where a temperature of 70° to 80°F can be maintained. If you have carried the fabric to the bottom of the dish, it can easily be kept wet by pouring a little water in the side of the dish. Don't disturb the seeds or use too much water, which may cause the seeds to mold.

As the seeds start to germinate, they should be removed to keep them from drying out the paper or the fabric and spoiling the tests of the slower seeds. If mold appears in one area, scrape it off so that it will not spread, and start a new test of that seed batch in another dish.

Keep a record of each square, showing the number of seeds planted and the number germinated. From this you can compute the seeds' viability in percentages. Remember that some seeds take longer than others to germinate.

Peat pots are fine and economical for starting plants indoors. They will decompose when planted.

Saving Your Own Seeds. Although I have emphasized the advantages of hybrid seed, most of the hybrids will *not* come true from saved seeds. If you wish to save your own seeds, use "open-pollinated" varieties.

You can save corn seed from *Golden Bantam, Country Gentleman*, and a white variety called *White Sunglow*. Note the nicest ears and mark the plants with a scrap of bright cloth or plastic. If your patch is troubled

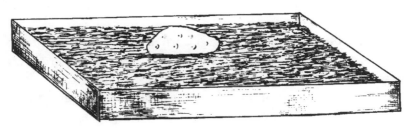

Sterilize transplanting or potting soil in a slow oven. It takes about the same amount of time it takes to bake a medium-sized potato.

with predators, fasten a mesh bag around the ears. Let the ears remain on the plants until late fall, then bring them indoors and store them in a dry place or hang them up by the husks as a decoration.

I especially like a variety of okra called *Gold Coast,* and because it is the only kind I plant, I can save the dry, mature pods for several years, occasionally buying fresh seed and starting over if it is cross-pollinating with varieties in neighboring gardens.

Egyptian onions, which are winter-hardy and very useful for flavoring soups and stews, produce both flowers and bulbs when in "blossom." The bulbs are really tiny plants and may be pulled apart and planted individually. Garlic, too, produces bulbs instead of blossoms, whereas leeks form usable seeds.

I got my start with leeks simply by buying them at a grocery store, where they are sold with the roots still attached. I bought several bunches and planted them; they multiplied and I've had leeks ever since. There are a surprising number of vegetables you can start this way (such as Jerusalem artichoke), and if the tubers have not been treated to retard sprouting, you can even sprout your own sweet potatoes.

Preparing New Seeds for Storage. When you save your own seed, always pick out the very best of the crop, letting it get ripe — actually overripe — before harvesting. Wash the seeds carefully and thoroughly in plain water, then spread them out in a thin layer on a paper towel so it will soak up the excess moisture. Put the seeds in a shallow pan or dish to dry for 2 or 3 weeks more, stirring them occasionally to prevent molding. When thoroughly dry, place in labeled envelopes and store in jars as with leftover seeds.

Reseeding. In some instances you may wish simply to let your plants reseed themselves. Lettuce is a good reseeder, as are many of the herb plants such as dill, catnip, borage, and horehound. Many reseeded herbs transplant readily, and the new plants may be harvested or used throughout the garden to protect other vegetables from insects, which often are deterred by their scents.

Speeding Germination. We can learn much about ways of persuading seeds to germinate quickly from those excellent gardeners, the Japanese. Before a seed can sprout, it must absorb moisture. When this happens, the outer skin or shell becomes soft, and the germ or kernel swells and burst forth toward the surface, seeking light.

Normally the seed receives the necessary moisture from the earth or the seedbed, but the process takes time, no matter how damp the soil.

To avoid chance fertilization when saving open-pollinated corn seed, slip a large plastic bag over each plant when the tassels begin to form.

Presoaking the seed in water before planting speeds up the process of germination by as much as 1 or 2 days. This accelerated process also reduces the chance of the shoot being attacked by chewing insects. In the garden it reduces the chore of keeping new seed beds constantly moist.

Seed soaking is particularly helpful with large, hard seeds such as corn, cucumber, melon, pumpkin, and squash, but also may be used for carrots, turnips, and beets. Beans and lettuce both are strong sprouters so I never soak them, but just about everything else can benefit from the process.

Special Seed-Soaking Tips

I'd suggest you limit seed-soaking to no more than 8 hours for your first try. In later soakings, change the water on all seeds at least every 8 hours to discourage growth of bacteria. The addition of a little vinegar (about 1 teaspoon) to alternate soaking baths lowers the pH and eliminates many bacteria.

Hard-shelled seeds such as canna, okra, and sweet peas won't benefit much from presoaking unless the seed coating is notched or pierced. If you do this, be careful not to go deeper than the coat and to stay away from the "eye" of the seed. Remember, too, that seeds so treated become very vulnerable to infection. It is best to soak them no more than 8 hours after this operation and to plant them as soon as swelling becomes apparent.

Water is another important factor. If possible, use rainwater instead of treated tapwater. I think that seeds soaked in rainwater grow healthier, sturdier plants.

CHAPTER 6

Planning for Water

Among the major factors affecting plant growth — soil, water, and sun — the gardener can do little about the last but provide for full exposure or shade, as needed. When it comes to rain at the right time, modern gardeners are almost just as much at the mercy of the weather as the old timers were. But, soil and water conditions *can* be greatly improved.

Without question, rainwater is best; but, if you don't get rainwater when it is needed most, there are a number of different ways to overcome the handicap. Again, remember that all growth-inducing factors must be at the highest levels for maximum yields — and water is one of the most important.

Sprinklers

In early spring when my garden has just been planted and the plants are yet to emerge (and for a period afterward while they still are small), I prefer overhead watering, which seems to suit most of the cool-season crops very well. For this purpose we use an oscillating-type sprinkler, sometimes called a rainmaker. If you're going to buy a sprinkler and hose, be sure to choose a large-diameter hose because this determines the number of gallons that will be put out in an hour.

You even can get an automatic sprinkler equipped both with a water meter and a timer: You set the sprinkler to come on at a specific time, it waters at a given pressure and for the length of time you have set it, and then it shuts off. It's great for people who must be away from home during the day, but it doesn't allow for an unexpected rainstorm.

With overhead watering you need only place your sprinkler where its gentle, softly falling drops can cover the vegetables and wet the soil slowly and thoroughly. To determine how much water is falling, set a large can at the outer edge of the watering perimeter: An inch of water accumulated in the can means an inch has fallen on the soil and plants.

Overhead watering works fine in the cool of early spring, and again in late fall, but there are hazards to this method in the warmer summer period. Overhead watering can damage many warm-weather crops — especially melons, squash, and other vine crops. It may encourage mildew and be a major cause of skin crack on tomatoes.

If overhead watering is continued into hot weather, be sure to do it early enough in the day so that plants are dry by evening. This applies particularly to northern and eastern U.S. gardens, where foliage may not dry as quickly as it does in the warmer air of the U.S. south and southwest.

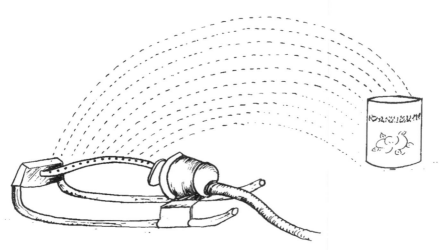

The output of an oscillating sprinkler can be measured by placing a can at the outer edge of the watered area.

Surface or Root Zone Watering

Even in the southwestern United States, we find overhead watering wasteful and impractical as the season advances. Especially on a windy day, a great deal of evaporation takes place before the water even hits the ground. If the day is sunny, there is further loss. This is when we turn to surface watering, also called "root zone" watering.

Although I now have accumulated various soakers, emitters, and spot-spitters, we once did a pretty good job just with an ordinary garden hose: We dug shallow trenches between the rows of the "hot-weather" vegetables — okra, tomatoes, peppers, eggplant, and squash — placed a soil barrier at each end, and filled the trench with old hay, leaves, and lawn clippings. When the hose was placed in the trench and the trench filled with water, the mulch floated to the surface then settled back again as the water soaked into the soil. The mulch helped greatly to retain the moisture over a longer period of time. When the corn was hilled, a natural trench was left between the rows, and if the weather turned dry, the trench was mulched and watered in the same way.

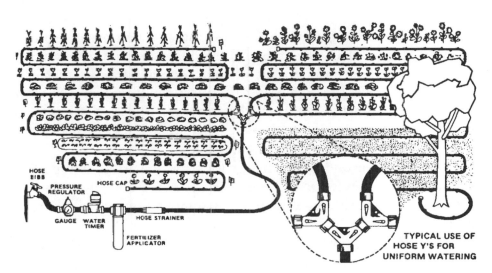

This surface irrigation setup can be timed to start itself and shut off. (Courtesy of Submatic Irrigation Systems)

Root Zone Irrigation

As water supplies become increasingly expensive and even limited for many, new systems are appearing on the market to give the root systems — and only the root systems — the water that they need for growth. This principle of making less water go further is something we all need to take into account when we design our gardens.

Root zone irrigation has been practiced for years in thousands of acres of orchards, nursery operations, and commercial row crops. The basic idea of root zone irrigation is to water every day but not too much, replacing *only* the moisture that the plant can use each day. By confining the moistened area to the plant's root zone, not only is there a dramatic saving in water, but weed growth is discouraged and nutrients are not so readily depleted from the soil.

There is still another advantage: Because the area is not wet to the point of saturation, the ground temperature is increased, which further stimulates plant growth. This can be an important factor in areas of limited sunshine.

Water Stress

A plant that is not receiving its necessary quota of water is under *water stress,* and this forces it to work harder as the moisture supply in the soil decreases. Water stress is progressive, and it may be slight to severe. Plants under stress — even large trees in a dry year — become more prone to insect damage than when they are growing well at a normal rate.

One important characteristic of root zone irrigation is that it is designed to prevent (as opposed to correct) a moisture stress. Most scientists now seem to agree that with "daily flow" irrigation, as it is often called, plants are not subjected to the moisture stresses that may cause them to stop growing or even wilt and die.

Although trees and shrubs may go for some time without water and not suffer unduly, water in the vegetable garden is absolutely necessary. Even a single day without water during a summer hot spell can ruin the entire garden.

Vegetables are affected by water stress in various ways. A cucumber plant under stress simply stops growing. When water is again supplied, the plant will resume growth if it has not been too long without moisture.

Potatoes tend to become knobby when watered in uneven amounts. Sweet corn is especially subject to water stress injury when it is tasseling. Root vegetables become woody and fibrous.

All vegetables, given the right combination of sunlight, air, and nutrients in the soil, seem to thrive on small amounts of water applied daily. If you must be away for any length of time, try to arrange for a gardening friend to take over — and you can do the same in return. Having a well-planned system will make this all less of a chore. You can choose between two main types of root zone water systems: drip irrigation or soaker hoses.

A Home-Garden Drip System

The most necessary item in a drip irrigation system for home gardens is the emitter. These small orifice fittings plug into a flexible type of polyethylene or vinyl hose.

They usually are spaced about every 1 to 2 feet in the hose, and then the hose is laid down by each row of plants. Because water drips out through the minute outlets, the water must be very clean so it doesn't plug up the tiny holes: It is usually passed through filters before being distributed in the system. The hose can be laid under the ground, but for ease of tilling, most gardeners prefer to have it on the top, where it can be easily removed at the end of the season when it is time to work the soil. You can even water your trees, shrubs, and containers with this kind of system.

In planning your system, it is important to determine how much of your garden area can be watered at one time. With emitters spaced every 2 feet, each 100-foot length of hose uses about 1 gallon of water per minute. If you are uncertain how much water your supply can deliver, see how long it takes to fill a 1-gallon container at the end of a garden hose. If it takes 10 seconds, then you have about 6 gallons per minute (the average for an outside hose bibb). This should be sufficient for up to six 100-foot lengths of hose. If more is required, the system should be divided into two or more sets and only one set watered at one time.

Soaker Hoses

These rubber hoses have tiny holes that allow water to seep out and into your soil. You can lay the hose down on top of the soil or bury it. Soaker hoses are not as elaborate as drip systems, but you can customize a soaker hose layout, and they are all you really need for a small, level garden.

How Long Do You Need To Water?

This depends to some extent on your type of soil. Soil improvement is discussed in Chapter 7. What I'm talking about here are soil *types*.

Gardening books always advise planting in "well-drained, rich, loamy soil" or state that a plant "does best in light, well-drained soil." What this really means is that the plant is easily damaged by too much water. It's not that complicated. You soon will know what type of soil you have by working with it, and you will water according to its composition. Clay soils have a high water-holding capacity. The air spaces in such soils are minute, and water moves through them slowly, so they usually need less water. Dig down with a spade occasionally to look at and feel such soil several inches beneath the surface.

The very best way to solve the problem of water management is to prepare a garden soil that can't be overwatered. In my opinion, this is best done by adding plenty of organic material. Plant roots require both moisture and air for growth. They need a growing medium that air can move through, bringing oxygen for their growth and removing the carbon dioxide they respire.

If the supply of air is stopped by filling all the air spaces in the soil with water, the root growth will stop. The longer the air is cut off, the greater the damage, and since damaged roots have little defense against rot-causing soil organisms, the plant dies.

We'll assume that you have improved your soil to the point where the water received is of greatest benefit. (Note the chart entitled *Water Retention* that follows.) One way to determine how much water is needed is by estimating the amount of daily evaporation loss in your area, for there is a correlation between the amount of water evaporated into the atmosphere and the amount used by plants. Replacement of 70 percent of the water that is evaporated each day should be adequate for most plants.

Tensiometers measure the soil moisture and are helpful, but you can get a pretty fair idea of what is going on by simple observation. On days of warm sun and high wind, there is more evaporation than on a day when it is cool, damp, and still.

There are systems that can be completely automated with solenoid valves, timers, and tensiometers, and that turn the system off when it rains or is too wet. Most gardeners favor accessories attached with garden hose threads (making it easy to add or remove any item without special tools). These accessories include valves, tees, strainers, filters, pressure gauges, pressure regulators, flow controls, and a variety of other items that can make root zone irrigation a very useful and convenient aid to gardening.

Even the small-plot gardener will find it is wise to select surface irrigation as the best method of applying water. When a large variety of vegetables is crowded into a small area, overhead sprinkling cannot be selective enough to avoid vegetables averse to water on foliage or fruit. And most of us, either through impatience or lack of time, are apt to underwater with a sprinkler.

Laying Out Your System

In laying out your irrigation system, try to keep the furrows as level as possible. Too much of an incline may cause the water to flow too rapidly and penetrate the soil unevenly. If your garden area is on a slope, choose a drip irrigation system that compensates for pressure changes — such as Netafim. Check-dams built with soil or boards also slow up the water flow and allow it to seep deeply into the soil.

Soil–Water Retention and Plant Use

As mentioned earlier, the available water-holding capacity of a soil depends primarily on the soil's texture. The *Water-Holding Capacity* table gives the approximate capacity of various soil types.

The soil depth from which a plant normally extracts water depends on the rooting depth of a plant, and the root depth varies with the type of plant. However, as a general guide, the main root zones of plants are as follows:

    ❦ Lawn grasses and leafy vegetables — top 1 foot
    ❦ Corn, tomatoes, and small shrubs — top 1 to 2 feet
    ❦ Small trees and large shrubs — top 2 or 3 feet

The amount of water a plant uses in 1 day depends on air temperature and wind velocity. The *Plant Water Use* table, based on location, serves as a guide to show inches of water the plant uses per cubic foot of soil that

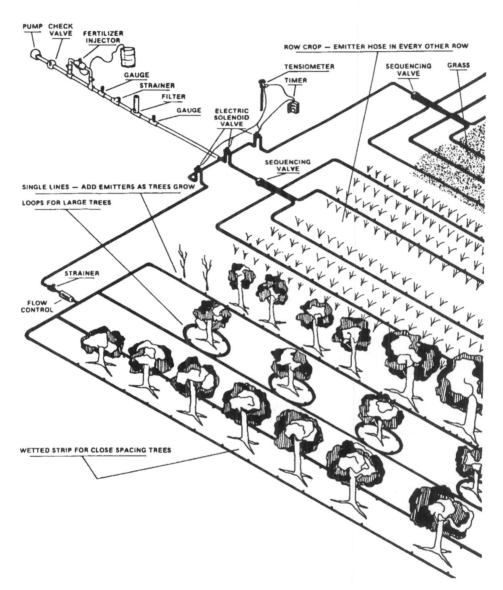

This subsurface emitter irrigation system includes a tensiometer to provide water only when the soil calls for it. (Courtesy of Submatic Irrigation Systems)

its root system covers. Remember that water use is slightly higher during dry, windy periods or when temperatures are abnormally high.

Water-Holding Capacity of Soil

Soil Types	Water in Inches Per Foot of Soil Depth	Gallons Per Cubic Foot of Soil
Sandy	0.8	0.5
Loam	1.6	1.0
Clay	2.4	1.5

Plant Water Use According to Irrigation and Location

| Irrigation Season | Location | |
	Southern or Southwestern States	Northern or Eastern States
Summer	0.25 to 0.35 in.	0.15 to 0.2 in.
Spring or fall	0.1 to 0.2 in.	0.1 to 0.15 in.

Gauging by Appearance. You can use plant symptoms, too, as a guide to water need. When short of water, many plants show a dark bluish-green color, wilt, or both. The symptoms first appear during the hottest part of the day.

Provide enough water at *each* irrigation to fill the soil reservoir for the plants to use over a period of time. It is best to give a thorough soaking, then not irrigate again until necessary.

Deep-rooted trees and shrubs can wait longer between irrigations, but you should apply two to three times as much water per irrigation as when watering more often. Small amounts of water result in excessive evaporation without deep wetting in the root zone, and this may result in excessive build-up of salts. A good rule is to irrigate plants thoroughly but not frequently.

CHAPTER 7

Fertile Soil Is Essential

Soil fertility is important for all gardening, but it requires special attention to achieve high yields in small spaces.

Soil fertility is affected by a soil's pH, which refers to how acid or alkaline the soil is. The pH ranges from 1 (pure acid) to 14 (pure alkaline); a pH of 7 is considered neutral. At certain pH levels some nutrients dissolve quickly into solution and can be used by plants; at other pH levels those same nutrients are insoluble. And plants have their pH preferences, too. Most garden crops grow best at a pH of between 6.5 and 6.9.

The knowledgeable gardener finds out whether the soil is acid or alkaline and by how much. There is really only one reliable way to find out your soil's pH — soil testing. Few of us are fortunate enough to have a perfect sandy loam, well endowed with organic matter. A soil test tells what type of soil you do have, what plants grow best in it, and how it may be improved. In general, sulfur is added to soil that is too alkaline, and lime is added to soil that is too acid.

Soil Testing

There are two ways to find out just what nutrients your soil may be hungry for: One way (and for a very nominal sum) is to have a test

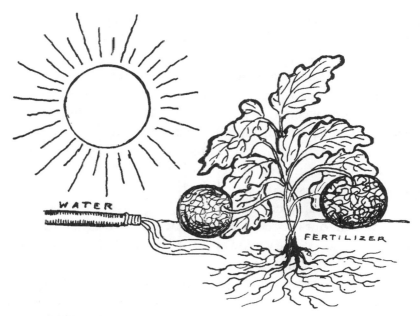

Adequate sun, rich soil, and ample moisture are needed for the fast vegetable growth that produces superior quality.

performed by your state university's College of Agriculture (details may be obtained from your County Extension Agent). Some universities now also give information especially tailored to organic gardeners.

Another way is to buy a soil testing kit and make the necessary tests yourself (or use both methods to doublecheck the results). With a good home testing kit (see *Sources of Supply* in Appendix), you can make periodic tests. This is a good idea because, although soil "looks" very similar from one season to the next, the nutrient supplies sometimes vary greatly.

Collecting Samples. Collecting the soil sample is your first and most critical step. How deeply you dig and the implement used depend on what you are going to plant. If you are testing the soil for planting fruit or nut trees, a soil auger or probe gives the best results, but if you are testing for a vegetable garden, an ordinary spade suffices.

The soil sample submitted for analysis should weigh about 1 pound, although only a small portion of it will be tested. For a vegetable garden, sink your spade in three or four different spots, digging down 6 to 7 inches. Take small cores from the center of each spadeful, put them in a clean quart jar, and mix together. Be sure your shovel and jar haven't been contaminated by a fertilizer.

Soil is easier to sample and handle when it is moist, so you might take a sample in early spring when the ground is too wet for plowing or tilling. Clay soil that is too wet may dry into hard clods, so break them up before they dry out. If you perform your own test, wait until the soil is fairly dry.

If you plan to send your soil sample to be tested, label it with your name, address, and the area from which it was taken. If your County Extension Agent doesn't have facilities for testing, she or he will know where to send the sample.

When you fill out the soil test forms, be sure to indicate the use you intend for the land. Whether you plan to plant trees or vegetables makes a difference in the recommendations you'll receive.

The soil is tested by putting a portion of the sample in a test tube and introducing one or two reagents, which react with the nutrient being tested and change color to show the quantity of nutrient available. If you are performing the test yourself, you compare the nutrient's color on the chart supplied with the test kit with that of the solution in the tube.

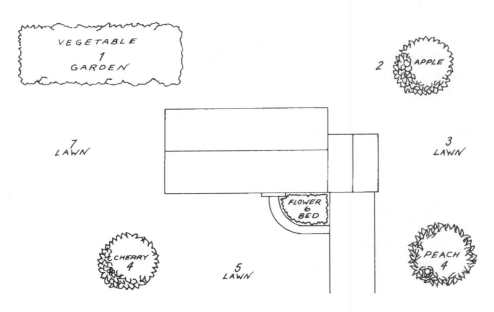

Gather samples for soil testing from different sections of the property — seven are suggested here — and have them tested separately for special planting plans.

pH Preferences of Vegetables, Fruit Trees, and Field Crops

Lime works as a team with fertilizers to produce high yields of better-quality crops. However, liming without adequate fertilization is seldom sufficient for satisfactory growth. Conversely, fertilizers are most soluble and available to plants when the pH is between 6.5 and 6.9. Soil bacteria also are most active in this range.

pH Preferences of Lawn Grasses

Bentgrass	5.5–6.5
Bermudagrass	5.0–7.0
Bluegrass, annual	5.0–7.5
Bluegrass, Canada	5.5–7.5
Bluegrass, Kentucky	6.0–7.5
Bluegrass, roughstock	5.5–7.5
Buffalograss	6.0–8.5
Carpetgrass	4.5–7.0
Centipedegrass	4.0–6.0
Clover, white	5.5–7.0
Fescue, chewings	5.5–7.5
Fescue, creeping red	5.5–7.5
Fescue, tall	5.5–7.5
Gramagrass	6.0–8.5
Redtop	5.0–7.5
Ryegrass	5.5–8.0
St. Augustine grass	6.0–8.0
Wheatgrass	6.0–8.5
Zoysia	4.5–7.5

(Courtesy of Sudbury Laboratories, Inc.)

Amount of Liming Materials Required to Raise pH Value 1 Unit

Soil	Ground Limestone, Marl, or Oyster Shells (Lbs. Per 100 Sq. Ft.)	Burnt Lime (Lbs. Per 100 Sq. Ft.)	Hydrated Lime (Lbs. Per 100 Sq. Ft.)
Light sandy	3	2	2½
Sandy loams	4½	2½	3⅓
Loams	6¾	3¾	5
Silt loams and clay loams	8	4½	6

Note: For soils low in organic matter, reduce the above amounts by 25%; for soils high in organic matter, increase by 100%.

Major Natural Sources of Nitrogen

One of the easiest and most effective ways to add nitrogen is by growing and turning under foliage crops. These "green manure plants" are also among the best soil conditioners. If you don't have time to make enough compost for your entire area, plant green manure crops such as clover, alfalfa, vetch, cowpea, buckwheat, or ryegrass.

Nitrogen, which is highly soluble and subject to rapid leaching, increases the protein content of food and feed crops and also feeds soil microorganisms during decomposition. It must be replaced frequently to maintain productivity.

Major Natural Sources of Phosphorus

When soil pH is below 5.0 and above 7.3, phosphorus locks up and becomes unavailable to plant roots. A shortage of this vital constitutent of every living cell (without it there would be no life) usually results in unsatisfactory plant growth.

Amounts To Use for Each 2%
of Nitrogen Needed

Material	Nitrogen (%)	Apply Per 100 Sq. Ft.	Apply Per Acre
Bloodmeal	15.0	10 oz.	265 lbs.
Felt wastes	14.0	12 oz.	285 lbs.
Hoofmeal/Horndust	12.5	13 oz.	320 lbs.
Guano	12.0	14 oz.	335 lbs.
Animal tankage	8.0	1¼ lbs.	500 lbs.
Cottonseed meal	8.0	1¼ lbs.	500 lbs.
Fish scraps	8.0	1¼ lbs.	500 lbs.
Milorganite (activated sludge)	6.0	1⅝ lbs.	665 lbs.
Castor pomace	5.5	1¾ lbs.	725 lbs.
Bonemeal	4.0	2½ lbs.	1,000 lbs.
Peanut shells	3.6	2¾ lbs.	1,100 lbs.
Tobacco stems or powder	3.3	3 lbs.	1,200 lbs.
Cowpea/Vetch/ Alfalfa hay	3.0	3⅝ lbs.	1,450 lbs.
Cocoa shells	2.7	3¾ lbs.	1,500 lbs.

Note: Most of these nitrogen sources also supply varying amounts of phosphorus or potash. For example, bonemeal contains 24 percent phosphorus.

(Courtesy of Sudbury Laboratories, Inc.)

Amounts To Use for Each 2% of Phosphorus Needed

Material	Phosphorus (%)	Apply Per 100 Sq. Ft.	Apply Per Acre
Phosphate rock	30.0	¾ lb.	270 lbs.
Bonemeal, steamed	28.0	¾ lb.	280 lbs.
Bonemeal, raw	24.0	⅞ lb.	330 lbs.
Animal tankage	20.0	1 lb.	400 lbs.
Fish scraps, dried	13.0	1¾ lbs.	675 lbs.
Basic slag	8.0	2½ lbs.	½ ton
Sugar wastes, raw	8.0	2½ lbs.	½ ton
Incinerator ash	5.0	4 lbs.	¾ ton
Milorganite (activated sludge)	3.0	7 lbs.	1¼ tons
Cottonseed meal	2.5	8 lbs.	1½ tons

Note: Some of these phosphorus sources also supply nitrogen or potash.

(Courtesy of Sudbury Laboratories, Inc.)

Major Natural Sources of Potash

Potash imparts increased vigor, disease resistance, winter hardiness, and strong, stiff stalks to plants. It is essential to the formation and transfer of starches, sugars, and oils.

Plant Food Sources Supplying More Than One Element

The materials listed in the chart entitled *Amount of Major Elements in Some Common Materials* comprise many trace elements. When raw organic matter is used, turn it under several weeks before planting. Leaves, alfalfa, and straw decompose much more quickly if ground up.

Amount To Use for Each 2% of Potash Needed

Material	Potash (%)	Apply Per 100 Sq. Ft.	Apply Per Acre
Flyash	12	14 oz.	335 lbs.
Wood ashes	8	1¼ lbs.	500 lbs.
Greensand	7	1½ lbs.	570 lbs.
Tobacco stems, powder	7	1½ lbs.	570 lbs.
Granite dust	5	2 lbs.	800 lbs.
Seaweed	5	2 lbs.	800 lbs.
Fish scrap, dried	4	2½ lbs.	1000 lbs.

Note: Some of these potash sources also supply nitrogen or phosphorus.

Natural Nutrients

When you have the results of your test, there are a number of things you can do to improve your soil. Even if you are not the dedicated organic gardener I am, you will find many sound reasons for using natural materials to build up the soil to the level necessary for intensive gardening. First, organic fertilizers usually cost little or nothing. Second, nothing can take the place of organic matter to improve your soil's texture.

Manure. Although not as easy to come by today, especially in a city or a suburb, manure is still one of the very best materials to use in your compost. But where are you going to get it? You probably won't be able to get it unless there is a racing stable, a cattle feed lot, or a commercial rabbit or poultry farm nearby where manure can be had for a small sum or free for the hauling.

It is inadvisable to use manure in its fresh state; it should be thoroughly decomposed through the composting process before it is placed on the vegetable garden. The value of manure varies according to the animal source and the food that the animal has received. (The

Amount of Major Elements in Some Common Materials

Material	Nitrogen (%)	Phosphorus (%)	Potash (%)
Activated sludge	6.0	3.0	—
Alfalfa hay	2.5	0.5	2.0
Animal tankage	8.0	20.0	—
Bloodmeal	15.0	1.0	0.5
Bonemeal	4.0	24.0	—
Castor pomace	5.5	1.5	1.0
Cocoa shells	2.7	1.5	2.7
Coffee grounds (dried)	2.0	0.3	0.5
Cottonseed meal	8.0	2.5	1.5
Fish scraps	8.0	13.0	4.0
Greensand	—	1.5	7.0
Guano	12.0	8.0	3.0
Hen manure (fresh)	1.6	1.5	1.0
Hoofmeal/Horndust	12.5	1.5	—
Horse/Cattle manure (fresh)	0.3	—	0.3
Incinerator ash	0.2	5.0	2.0
Seaweed	1.5	1.0	5.0
Sheep manure (fresh)	0.5	0.3	—
Tobacco stems, powder	3.3	—	7.0
Wood ashes	—	1.5	8.0

manure of older animals is richer than that of younger ones.) The table that follows gives good approximations of the value of manure from different farm animals.

Garden crops, especially root crops, respond very favorably to generous applications of composted manure. However, caution should be used with potatoes. Even if well-decomposed manure is used, it should be plowed or raked well under the topsoil the autumn before a spring planting.

Garbage. There are a lot of other fine organic materials you can use.

Percentages of Nitrogen, Phosphate, and Potash in Different Manures

Species of Animal	Nitrogen (%)	Phosphate (%)	Potash (%)
Rabbit	2.4	1.4	0.6
Poultry (chickens)	1.1	0.8	0.5
Sheep	0.7	0.3	0.9
Steer	0.7	0.3	0.4
Horse	0.7	0.3	0.6
Duck	0.6	1.4	0.5
Cow	0.6	0.2	0.5
Pig	0.5	0.3	0.5

For starters, put your own garbage to work by placing it in your compost bin or burying it directly in the planting row.

If you don't want to bury it directly in the garden, which involves digging a hole each time, a pre-dug pit is a simple and quick method. It's really best to dig two pits, each 2 feet deep by 3 feet wide and long, and frame them with rocks or boards on three sides that rise about 8 inches above ground level. Cover with a heavy wooden lid.

Work the pits alternately. Dump the garbage and layer it with soil and green crop residues; even weeds, which contain many minerals, add greatly to soil fertility. Turn your first pile several times and then leave it to mature while you work with the second pit. Of course, you can build a compost heap above the ground, but the pit method keeps it out of sight, keeps down odors, and keeps out animals. If you need more compost, just increase the size or number of your pits.

Leaves and Clippings. If you don't have a shredder, here is a way you can use your own (and neighbors') leaves and lawn clippings. Raise your rotary lawn mower about 4 inches on a platform built of 2x4s. The frame should be solid, the mower wheels blocked, and care taken in starting the machine. Pile leaves near the outside of the propped-up mower, start it, and sweep up a rakeful of leaves. As they are sucked through the blades and ejected through the chute, they will make a heap

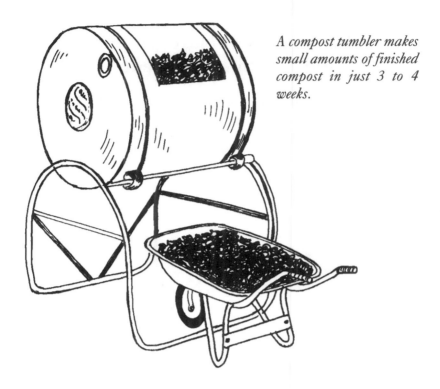

A compost tumbler makes small amounts of finished compost in just 3 to 4 weeks.

of fine mulch that is about one-tenth the size of the original pile and just right for composting.

Lawn clippings — yours and your neighbors' — may be treated in the same way as leaves to make rich compost. In the summer, clippings can be applied in a thin layer (so they will not heat) as mulch between your garden rows to conserve moisture and inhibit weeds. As they gradually break down, adding fertility to the soil, keep adding more.

Other Organic Wastes. In a city area many other organic wastes often can be found that are greatly beneficial when added to compost piles. Buckwheat hulls, cocoa bean wastes, and peanut shells have been available commercially for many years. Now, many other wastes are being discovered. Some of these represent sources of organic matter; others furnish needed minerals to the soil.

A list of these wastes includes apple pomace, banana residue, basic slag, beet waste, brewery waste, castor pomace, citrus waste, coffee waste, cotton gin waste, garbage, grape pomace, leather dust, nutshells, peanut hulls, pea waste, potato waste, rice hulls, seaweed, silk mill waste, tobacco waste, and wood waste, such as sawdust or wood chips.

You can build an outdoor pile or contain your debris in a wooden or wire bin. Plastic composters also are available, and they have the advantage of retaining heat and moisture for faster decomposition. Plastic compost tumblers, which turn to aid mixing of the materials, produce the quickest compost. For those who want more information on compost making and compost materials, read Stu Campbell's *Let It Rot!* (see in the Appendix under *Other Books From Storey Communications You'll Enjoy*).

This by no means exhausts the list, and in almost every part of the country there are waste products particular to whatever is grown or processed in the region. These often can be had free for the hauling.

Rock Powders for Soil Minerals

Your soil tests may reveal a deficiency in some important nutrients. For many soils, ground phosphate and granite rock do a good job of soil and plant nourishing without the addition of chemical forcing agents. Rock minerals and organic matter have an important relationship; the more organic matter there is in a soil, the more readily the ground rock goes to work. As the organic matter decays, mild acids (including carbonic acid) are produced that aid in dissolving the rock particles.

A 4 x 5-foot compost bin, perhaps with cover, can be tucked away on any suburban location.

Liming

Lime mixed into a stiff clayey soil makes it friable and more easily worked, lowers its plasticity, and reduces the adhesion of the particles, which promotes better drainage and texture. You'll find nothing better than a dressing of agricultural lime to improve a clay soil. Your soil will also be warmer, thus ensuring earlier cropping in spring and earlier maturity in fall. On the other hand, a loose sandy soil that dries too quickly is rendered more compact by the use of lime, more retentive of moisture, and better able to carry crops through a dry spell. Lime also acts chemically on heavy soils, setting free the potash that otherwise would be unavailable to plants. It is a soil tonic and effectively counteracts conditions of acidity under which many vegetables won't grow well.

The efficiency of lime depends on its even distribution and good mixture with the soil. In a level garden, broadcast lime onto the surface of newly dug soil in late winter or early spring so that the rains will wash it in. The dry residue is mixed in when the ground is prepared for sowing or planting.

Other Mineral Additives

A potassium soil deficiency probably can be corrected most quickly by the use of wood ashes. I save the ashes of all our tree prunings, as well as those from logs burned in the fireplace. You may spread ashes directly on your garden (if it is level) even if there is snow on the ground, or put them on your ripening compost or any leaves you may have stacked around awaiting disposal.

If you don't have wood ashes, buy some greensand. Cottonseed meal is also rich in nitrogen and has a good amount of potash, phosphorus, and the trace minerals, all of them quickly available. Unlike wood ashes, which raise the pH of the soil, cottonseed meal is acid in its reaction and lowers the pH. So, use either one according to your need. Bloodmeal is a very good source of nitrogen and bonemeal a good source of phosphorus.

A Big "Potting Soil" Operation

What about the soil you want to use in your raised beds? I discussed earlier how to dig these beds and incorporate organic materials and minerals. Now, let's suppose that you want to prepare the soil especially for a certain bed, say for a salad garden by the kitchen.

You can make your own planting mix, adjusting what you put in it to the herbs or vegetables you want to grow. You do this by working from the table of *pH Preferences* (see Appendix). Remember that whatever you put in should be thoroughly mixed so that each portion of the mix has the right proportions of each of the ingredients — something not easy to do by stirring with a large amount of soil.

Start with a pile of compost, peat moss, or good loamy garden soil. Or, if the soil you dug out of the bed is of reasonably good quality, you can use that. Have ready your bags of lime, cottonseed meal, or other materials. You may even want to mix in some sand or vermiculite to improve texture. Scatter the added materials as evenly as possible over the basic pile. Shoveling from this pile, start building a new cone-shaped heap, pouring each shovelful directly on top so that the soil dribbles down the sides. After you have repeated this operation at least three times, your materials will be thoroughly and evenly mixed and ready to fill your raised bed.

Making up a large quantity of garden soil for special beds: Mix the pile of ingredients thoroughly three times.

Keep on Building

Although you have corrected imbalances or mineral deficiencies in your soil and added abundant organic matter, you can't consider the job done, once and for all. Whether the soil is in a conventional garden or raised beds, you must *keep* it in a state of high fertility. You won't need to work as hard to do this, but be sure to test it from time to time to be certain the soil is still in good balance.

Most soils never seem to get enough organic matter, especially in areas where the intense sun rapidly decomposes the humus. I've been adding compost to our hardpan soil for 30 years and don't dare stop, but it's in such prime condition now that it will grow just about anything, and I intend to keep it that way.

CHAPTER 8

————•◦❧◦•————

The Tools You Need

Don't be frightened away from gardening because you think you need to buy lots of tools. You can make do with just a few, initially. In time you will know how much garden space to allocate and whether you will garden in conventional or raised beds. Your available time, physical strength, and personal feelings about digging are also important considerations. So, it's probably best to start small and see what you really need.

A Tiller?

The first year you might want to rent a tiller to break ground and mix the soil. But don't start too big. Remember that a small garden, carefully kept, will yield more than a large, weedy one. The first year, too, your supply of compost may not be large enough to cover a wide area, but as you increase the fertility of your soil, your garden space can grow.

Basic Tools

First, buy a good D-handle spade that is strong and sturdy, because you will be using it in many garden jobs for years to come. Actually, you can get by with just a spade and a hoe for a very small garden the first year or two.

Next, I would buy a flat-tined spading fork, a long-handled pointed shovel, an iron rake, a bent-fork weeder, a sturdy trowel, a wheelbarrow or garden cart, and garden shears. If you decide to keep part of your area in lawn, you also need a mower. I'd recommend a small rotary power mower for its ability to shred compost.

In time you will need a pair of good loppers for heavy pruning (especially if you plan to grow fruit trees), and perhaps a sprayer. You can borrow from your kitchen things such as a paring knife, a plastic bucket, and twine.

You can make tools that are handy for special purposes and improvise things such as garden stakes (for example, we use discarded auto shock absorbers). To help keep watch on insects on my garden plants, for instance, I mounted a small mirror on a pancake turner, which lets me see without bending or stooping the undersides of the leaves where infestations can start.

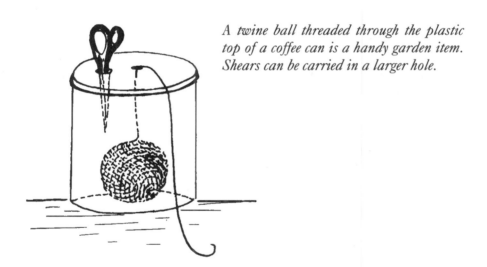

A twine ball threaded through the plastic top of a coffee can is a handy garden item. Shears can be carried in a larger hole.

Shovels and Forks. Your spading fork or long-handled shovel is useful for digging or spading up the ground. The long-handled shovel (not too heavy — perhaps No. 9) gives you leverage for digging holes for planting trees or shrubs and is also useful for broadcast spreading of compost over a garden area or adding compost to a seeding furrow.

A long-toothed iron rake is useful for cultivating and preparing a seed bed, mixing compost into the surface, and hilling (such as drawing earth over a side dressing of compost). A bow or lawn rake is useful for preparing smooth seed beds, raking small stones and sticks out of the way, or for gathering leaves, weeds, and other organic material you want to put on your compost heap.

Hoes and Hoeing. Hoes come in various types. Besides the usual flat-bladed hoes, there is also a pointed hoe that is particularly useful in the very small garden and allows you to make a furrow of the required depth when planting.

However, the flat-bladed hoe is used for most cultivating jobs, so select with care. A big, heavy hoe is tiring to swing, so the lighter the hoe, the better. Also consider the thickness of the handle in relation to the size of your own hands: It should be comfortable to hold with or without gloves.

Hoe length is important, too: It should be just long enough for you to grasp almost at the end and still be able to stand nearly straight and chop. When I was first married, my short-handled hoe was a great family joke. I would tell my friends, "I am sure my husband loves me, he even cut the hoe handle off short to help me chop weeds!" This was always good for a laugh, but it was the truth. The longer the handle, the less your leverage on the blade. If the handle comes to the middle of your chest, it will be just about right.

How you use your hoe when weeding also makes a great difference. To be effective, you must destroy the weeds' root system as well as the part seen on the surface. You can do this without getting tired if you tip your hoe blade to one side. This means that (starting on the right side of your row) you tip the blade so that the right corner strikes the ground first. Then, chopping in an arc from one side of the row to the other and with short and easy strokes, bring your blade into contact with the ground as close to flat as possible.

With each stroke, your blade edge should stop about 2 inches under the surface and should travel about 6 inches through the soil. On your way back down the row, you should reverse this process so the left corner of your blade hits the ground first. Tipping your blade causes it to slide under the ground more easily and saves you a surprising amount of energy. It is much more effective, too, than hitting the weeds head on. The triangular or pointed hoe is particularly adapted for working close to the rows and is also handy for raised beds in which vegetables are planted very close together.

Trowels. Trowels, used for lifting seedlings for transplanting and making holes for small plants, come in many types; each is useful for a special purpose. A broad trowel is good for lifting plants with fairly large

To save blisters, add a rubber grip to your hoe handle.

root systems, transplanting, and digging larger holes. The smaller, narrower trowel is the best one to make a hole for a little plant. Hold the trowel against the side of the hole, insert the plant with the roots hanging down, and push the soil up to the roots with the trowel. Then slip out the trowel and firm the earth around the stem with your fingers.

Buy sturdy trowels. Those that attach to their handles with crimped metal soon bend and break.

The many types of hand forks and weeders are all useful for cultivating around young plants. A three-fingered weeder, either with long or short handle, is particularly handy. There also is a hand fork with flat tines that is useful for loosening soil around the roots of larger plants.

Moving Things

You'll need to move bulky materials — bales of hay or bags of leaves or lawn clippings — and maybe loads of soil mix. The usual choice, the wheelbarrow, is a back-breaking device that is mainly useful if heavy loads must be moved on lanes so narrow that only one wheel can pass. A far better choice is a two-wheeled cart, which balances its own load without using your back as a fulcrum. Before you buy a wheelbarrow, investigate the modern two-wheeled carts, particularly those with wheels big enough to carry the load through soft soil or on grassy lawns.

Other Tools

If you decide to plant a small orchard, you may want a few other tools (besides your loppers), such as a pole pruner, a pruning saw, pruning shears, and a pruning knife. But most of these are not needed while your trees are still small.

Many gardeners find the wheel hoe or walking cultivator handy for the small plot. This tool was the source of another family joke years ago. My husband, Carl, worked long, hard hours and often arrived home quite late. To get in a few hours of garden work after dark he attached a flashlight to the wheel hoe — a picture the family will never forget!

We still have that wheel hoe and sometimes use it for small jobs. It has undergone many changes and several new sets of wooden handles. The metal wheel has been replaced with one from a discarded bicycle. But, the old framework is still there and probably will last for many more years.

Tool Care

Don't fail to give your tools good care, including proper storage, for when left in the open and exposed to weather, they soon deteriorate. Plan for a small toolshed or space in your garage where they can be kept in good order.

Use tools for the jobs for which they were designed. If soil is too hard for a trowel, for example, use a spade or shovel. Use a hand pruner on branches small enough to cut easily; use grass shears on grass and not on

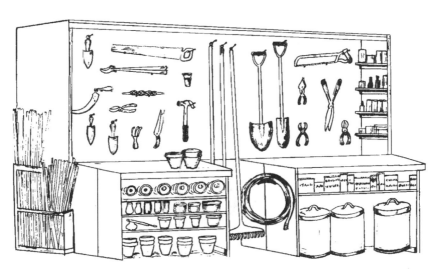

Even minigardening is easier and more fun if you have a well-ordered tool and storage area for supplies and implements.

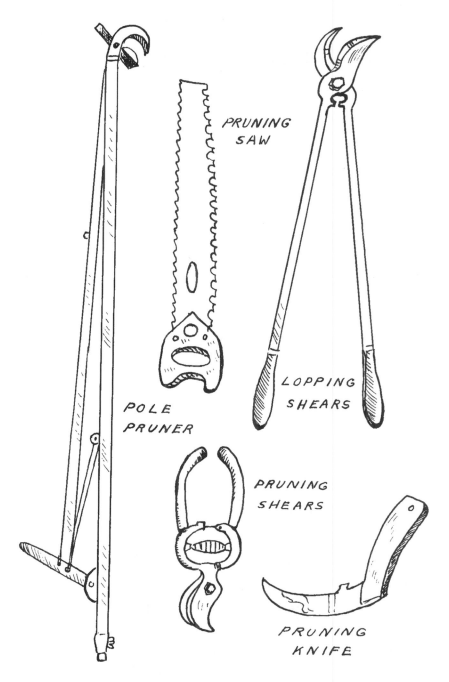

PRUNING
SAW

POLE
PRUNER

LOPPING
SHEARS

PRUNING
SHEARS

PRUNING
KNIFE

These pruning tools, perhaps with a portable hand sprayer included, take care of shrub and fruit tree work.

weeds. Don't use your trowel to pry rocks loose or a shovel's back as a hammer.

A dull hoe blade can make your gardening work twice as hard. Lock the blade in a vise and sharpen with a coarse, flat file. Place the file on a beveled, 45° angle to the blade, and stroke toward the handle. If you move in this fashion and take your time, you won't be apt to slice off a finger if your hands slip.

Always clean your tools after each use, for moisture and soil rust and corrode the metal surfaces. Keep a putty knife handy to clean shovels and trowels. At the end of each day's use, wipe a film of oil on the metal parts with a piece of burlap or other rough cloth. For quick protection, plunge your tools into a bucket of oily sand kept for this purpose.

Besides your shovels and hoes, the tools with cutting blades, such as shears, should be kept sharp; for overwinter storage, apply a heavy oil film or rust inhibitor. Store your tools in a dry place indoors in an orderly way so you can find them or know if they are lost or misplaced.

One of the first things I do with a new tool is to paint the handles a bright orange. This is a tremendous help, especially when the small ones are mislaid in the garden: They gleam brightly even in tall grass and no time is wasted in hunting for them.

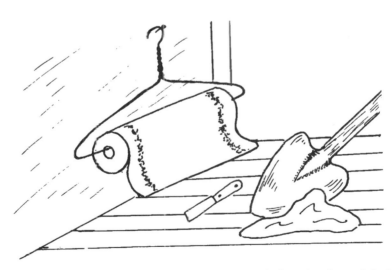

Always clean tools after use. A roll of paper towels kept in the toolshed allows easy drying after you wash the tools.

CHAPTER 9

❖

Dwarf Fruit Trees for Small Spaces

Dwarf trees seldom are planted on a small lot in the form of an orchard; rather, they are included as a part of the overall landscape. Yet, you can grow enough fruit on dwarf trees to make them very worthwhile.

Dwarf fruit trees have come a long way; they are constantly being improved and new varieties introduced. You can expect a yield of about 2 bushels per year; even 3 bushels isn't uncommon from a dwarf apple tree, and some of the very thrifty spur-types occasionally have astonished home gardeners with a yield of as much as 6 bushels! Many growers believe dwarf trees make more efficient use of soil nutrients than standard trees: The fruit is as big or bigger than that of standard trees and of the finest quality.

Dwarf trees come in sizes from those small enough to grow in box planters to semi-dwarfs, which are about two-thirds as tall as standard fruit trees. All have a healthy, long life.

Some fruit trees, such as the *North Star* cherry, are genetic dwarfs. Others are dwarfed by grafting a standard fruit-bearing top onto the rootstock of a natural dwarf so that the entire tree is dwarfed. This is the method most widely used by specialty nurseries (see the Appendix, under *Sources of Supply*).

Dwarf fruit trees are especially valuable if you have little space; in fact, they may be your only possibility. But, even if you have a sizable piece of ground available — for example, 6,400 square feet — on which you could plant a dozen standard-sized trees, you could plant an average of 60 dwarf trees on it and your range of kinds and varieties would be far wider. This also gives you a margin of safety in case some of the varieties don't bear well some years.

Dwarfs often bear fruit the same year you plant them or the year after, particularly if you buy ones of bearing age. They are easy to care for — to spray, prune, or harvest — and do especially well when placed on a wall or framework, such as espaliers, which is another big plus for planting dwarf trees. It is wise to protect the ripening fruit from birds with nylon netting.

Choosing Your Dwarf Trees

Many of these trees, such as the dual-purpose peaches, are ornamental, too. *Stark Early White Giant* (best in Zones 5 to 8), *Com-Pact Redhaven* or *Belle of Georgia* easily fit into places too small for standard peaches. *Elberta, Madison,* and *Reliance* are other fine peach choices. *Stark Early White Giant* ripens first, in early summer, followed about 1 month later by *Reliance,* and in late summer by *Belle of Georgia.* Nectarines taste much the same as peaches but have the merit of being fuzzless. Try the dwarf *Stark Crimson Gold* and *Mericrest.*

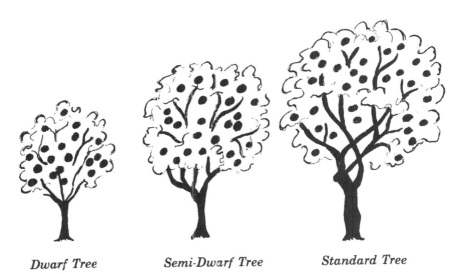

Dwarf Tree   Semi-Dwarf Tree   Standard Tree

Space-saving dwarf and semi-dwarf trees usually are best planted on the house lot and allow you to have more varieties in the same amount of space.

Many varieties of cherry trees provide showy blossoms and fine fruits. The sweet cherry types need two for pollination; sour cherries only need one.

If you live in a warm climate, you may want to try dwarf persimmons and figs, which I grow with no problems. For even more favorable areas, there also are citrus, guava, loquat, and papaya dwarf trees to consider.

Dwarf apple trees can be trained along walls or fences or even mixed in bilevel fashion with flower or vegetable patches. Good choices include *Red* and *Golden Delicious, Jonathan,* and *Lodi.*

Dwarf pear trees include *Bartlett, Moonglow, Seckel, Kieffer,* and *Harrow Delight;* dwarf plums offer a choice of *Burbank Red Ace, Ember,* and *Stanley;* in cherry dwarfs there are *Garden Bing, Northstar,* and *Meteor.*

When choosing trees (and be sure to order them early), remember that not all dwarfs are self-fertile, and some must be cross-pollinated by another variety planted nearby. These pollination requirements are detailed in my book *Carrots Love Tomatoes* (see the Appendix, under *Other Books From Storey Communications You'll Enjoy*).

Choosing Your Site

Before ordering your trees, draw in your choices on your lot plan (see Chapter 1), making sure to note neighboring shade and fruit trees and especially the open space each dwarf needs at maturity. Don't crowd — it is better to have one or two fine trees than several that are badly spaced.

Be sure to test for good soil drainage before you place the trees and avoid low-lying sections of land where cold air flow may kill early blossoms. Do not plant the trees in shade or near the roots of other trees.

Planting

Except for areas in which winters are severe, fall is the ideal time for setting out nearly all fruit trees. This allows young trees to acclimate and recover energy lost in transplanting before starting into spring growth.

A tree that arrives from the nursery balled and burlapped or container grown can be held for a short while before planting if conditions are suitable, but the bare-root stock should be "puddled" in a tub of thick, muddy water to prevent it from drying out. If spring trees arrive frozen, thaw them out gradually in a cold room.

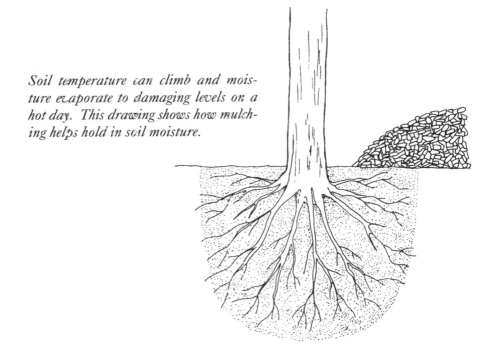

Soil temperature can climb and moisture evaporate to damaging levels on a hot day. This drawing shows how mulching helps hold in soil moisture.

Make planting holes large enough to receive the roots when they are spread out in a natural position. If trees are balled and burlapped, dig the hole at least 2 feet wider than the rootball. Take care to disturb as little as possible the roots or soil around them. Prune off any broken roots.

Rather shallow planting is best, particularly if the trees are to be staked, but dig deep enough so the top of the root ball is at ground level. The graft union visible on the trunk should be kept above the ground.

If you are planting several trees, keep their roots in a fold of wet burlap to prevent drying. If the soil is especially dry, dig the holes in advance and pour in two or more buckets of water. Refill the holes, packing in around the root systems with good topsoil or a mixture of loam, peat moss, and compost. Top with 2 to 4 inches of bark mulch, leaving about 2 inches around the trunk free of bark to serve as a water reservoir. Use no fertilizer now or during the first year.

Pruning and Staking

Newly planted 1- and 2-year-old trees generally should be pruned back, depending on the shape of tree desired. For small apple trees, simply thin out excess branches, and possibly shorten some shoots. Peach, nectarine, and sweet cherry trees should be pruned even more severely.

Tie the trees loosely with soft twine to stakes after planting and pruning. Wrap the trunks with foil, burlap strip, or creped kraft paper to prevent sunscald; protect against rodents with a cylinder of ¼-inch mesh hardware cloth set into the soil. Then mulch around the trees with hay or straw.

Insect Protection

After a long, cold winter we welcome the sun, and so do the insect eggs attached to your fruit trees. This is the time to apply your own or purchased dormant oil spray. The oil coats, penetrates, and suffocates the soft-bodied mite and scale eggs. (See the Appendix, under *Sources of Supply*.)

Some growers also find this spray effective against fireblight on pear trees. Do not use it on citrus. If you live in the southern or southwestern United States, it is a good idea to use the spray in the fall as well, after the leaves are off the trees and the temperature is above 40°F.

Making Your Own Spray. Dormant oil spray is easily made: Simply combine 1 gallon of light-grade oil and 1 pound of soap (preferably fish

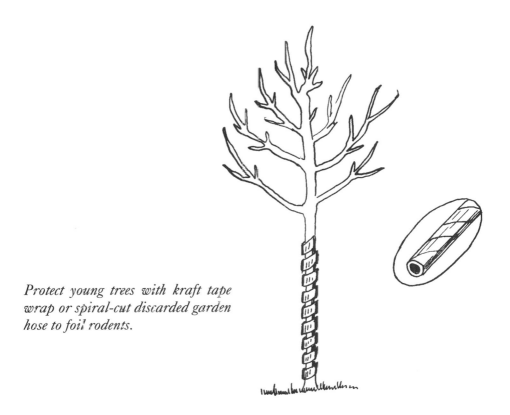

Protect young trees with kraft tape wrap or spiral-cut discarded garden hose to foil rodents.

oil soap, found in garden shops and some drugstores) with ½ gallon of water. Boil. Pour the mixture back and forth from one container to another until well blended. Dilute with 20 times its volume of water and use at once before it separates.

It's best to apply the spray when the buds begin swelling but before they open: The closer the spraying is to mite- and scale-hatching time, the more effective it will be. Tests have shown that more red spider mite eggs are killed at this later stage than when the weather is still severely cold and the eggs are hard.

Be sure to use a good sprayer and to coat all the limbs from the top to the bottom of your trees. Use it on all your fruit trees (except citrus) — peach, plum, apple, pear, and apricot. Don't worry about applying too much. The excess will run off, leaving a thin coating of oil to do the work. It is best to coat the whole tree before going on to the next one.

Dormant oil spray won't touch the pests that overwinter or lay eggs in the trash and leaves under apple trees, pupate in the ground, and fly up into the trees after the leaves have opened. The best prevention is to keep the ground clear of fallen fruit and leaves. This does not necessarily mean leaving the earth under your trees bare. A permanent mulch under the trees may provide a place for some of these pests to overwinter, but it also harbors their natural enemies, the ladybird beetles.

Nasturtiums planted under apple trees protect against woolly aphids, and sprays made from their leaves also are beneficial. I always plant garlic thickly around the trunks of the young peaches and plums in my small orchard as a protection against the borers that often attack them.

Later Care

It is important to keep the weed growth down around young trees, particularly during the first summer — either by cultivation or, preferably, by mulch (which feeds the surface roots as it decomposes). Use 3 to 6 inches of hay, compost, or other organic matter around the trees. Trees in hot and dry regions need particular attention to water. If rainfall is inadequate and the ground is very dry, soak it to a depth of at least 8 to 10 inches at least once a week.

Espaliered Trees

Espaliering is a method of training a fruit tree or shrub to grow on a trellis or a lattice, or against a wall (whose protection makes it possible to grow the trees in climates otherwise not favorable). This method has the added advantages both of being ornamental and of fitting a tree into a space where there otherwise would not be enough room. Dwarf apples and pears are favorites for growing this way (and in warm climates, figs).

Espaliered trees are not difficult to manage because they are well within reach for pruning, spraying, and harvesting (and produce fruit of very high quality), but success begins with buying a tree with a framework of branches already shaped by skilled nursery people. Espaliered trees should always be on a dwarfing rootstock. You may plant them in well-prepared soil in spring or autumn, as you would other dwarf trees.

Well-built suitable supports are necessary, and when trees are grown on a trellis or wire fence, the branches must be evenly spaced and securely fastened or they will become unshapely. When espaliered trees are grown against a wall or fence, wires should be stretched taut between

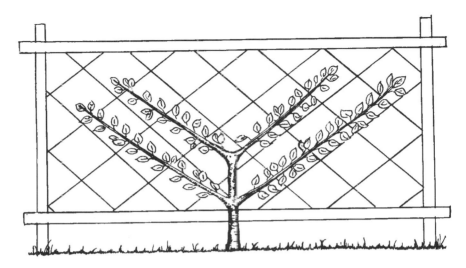

Espaliered fruit trees fit against walls and fences and take little garden space.

eyelet nails driven into the wood or brickwork, and held 4 or 6 inches out from the wall and about 1 foot apart. (Branches should not be fastened close against the bricks or wood.)

It may seem that strong supports are not needed at first, but you will save time later by erecting a permanent trellis with sturdy support posts for the wires.

If you are planting several trees, place smaller intermediary posts at intervals between the end posts. Set the bottom wire about 15 inches above ground level and the others at intervals of 1 foot above each other. The topmost wire should be about 5 feet above the ground, depending on the number of tiers of branches needed.

Espaliered Tree Pruning. As soon as your tree's leaves have fallen in autumn, give the tree its annual winter pruning by cutting back each side or lateral shoot (which develop along the horizontal branches) to within two or three buds of the base. The extension shoots at the end of each branch should be lightly tipped, but if they are very long, shorten them by one-third.

The spurs, which form along the main branches as a result of this pruning, should be kept 5 or 6 inches apart; as they become longer and multibranched, cut the spurs back and leave only three or four fruit buds on each.

Capsule Information on Fruit Tree Pollination

All fruit varieties are classed as self-fruitful, partially self-fruitful, or self-unfruitful (because of poor pollen). A self-fruitful variety bears well without another variety for pollination. If the variety is partially self-fruitful, it does not *need* another variety for pollination but bears more heavily if cross-pollinated. A self-unfruitful variety requires another variety for pollination.

Generally speaking, if a species is a good pollinator for one variety, it is a desirable cross for any other variety of the same fruit family. For example, the *Delicious* apple is an excellent pollinator planted with other apple varieties. However, a species of one family can never pollinate a species of another family (for example, an apple with a peach tree). Plant trees within a 50-foot radius to take care of pollination distance. Take into account any neighbors' trees.

Apple. Varieties may be self-fruitful or self-unfruitful; even with varieties classed as self-fruitful, you will have a better crop if two varieties are planted. *Cortland, Delicious, Rome, Yellow Delicious, Jonathan,* and *Wealthy* are good pollinators and may be used to set fruit for early, medium, or late varieties.

Pear. Most pear varieties require cross-pollination, but all bear excellent pollen and have proven to be effective pollinizers for each other. The exception is *Bartlett* and *Seckel* varieties, which are intersterile and require a third variety for fertilization to occur. As is the case with apples, it is best to plant two different varieties of pears.

Plum. There is variation in their needs according to species and variety. Most fall into one of two groups: European or Japanese. Although nearly all plum varieties require cross-pollination to fruit, these two species do not intercross freely. Plant two European or two Japanese plums to ensure a crop of fruit.

Peach and Nectarine. Most varieties are considered self-fruitful if planted alone. The most important exception is the *J.H. Hale* peach, which must be planted with another variety. Nectarines are self-fruitful and also pollinate peaches. Peaches planted nearby help nectarines to set a full crop.

Apricot. Most apricots are self-fertile but bear more heavily if cross-pollinated. *Moongold* and *Sungold,* two hardy hybrids, are companion varieties meant to be planted in pairs.

Cherry. All sour cherries are self-fruitful and bear well if planted alone. Good varieties are *Early, Richmond, Montmorency,* and *Meteor.* All sweet cherries are self-unfruitful and need another variety nearby to set fruit. *Black Tartarian* is recommended as the best pollinator.

CHAPTER 10

Shrubbery: Ornamental and Edible

Nuts, small fruits, and berries are valuable additions to a small property because of their dual roles. You may want vegetables neither in your front yard nor even semihidden among the flowers, but you might still like to have a display planting yield of something good to eat.

Consider the many fruiting bushes that are just as decorative as other shrubs used merely for landscaping purposes. You can enjoy fresh fruit; save some for jellies, jams, and wines; and freeze enough to last you all year.

Think about using low-growing shrubs as foundation plants to soften angles and hug the house. And, as a landscape accent, try a shrub with unusual foliage or one whose flowers or berries are especially attractive. A flowering crabapple provides apples to eat and with which to make delicious jelly. The dwarf variety of flowering quince, which stands up well under city conditions, yields yellow fruit good for preserves.

You may wish to plant a border as a small windbreak or "shelter belt" to protect your house. This is best accomplished with one or more rows of evergreens, but the effect can be lightened by interplanting with flowering and fruiting shrubs or by making one row of each. Use hedges to mark boundary lines, or taller-growing shrubs to screen out an

Capsule Information on Fruiting Shrubs for Yard and Kitchen

Height

American Highbush Cranberry *(Viburnum trilobum)*. Sparkling red berries, good for preserving, are preceded in spring by clusters of showy, hydrangea-like white flowers. Does well along shore lines, on slopes, in sun or shade. Plant 4 feet apart for hedge, 8 feet apart for individual plants.
    8–12 ft.

Autumn Olive *(Elaeagnus umbellata)*. Its dense, silvery green hedge is covered with berries that make a piquant jelly. Is good for a windbreak planting.
    6–10 ft.

Elderberry. Has large clusters of glistening black fruit. Is good for pies, wine, jelly, jams, and preserves. Attractive white flower clusters appear in June.
    5–6 ft.

European Cranberry *(Viburnum opulus)*. Rugged shrub with dark green, maple-shaped leaves and bright scarlet berries. Berries are sour but can be used to make a jelly that is high in vitamin C.
    6–8 ft.

Hansen's Bush Cherry. An improved form of the Western Bush Cherry, it produces white flowers followed by deep crimson fruit. Its silvery leaves form a dense screen.
    4–5 ft.

Hardy Beach Plum *(Prunus maritima)*. Thrives well on poor soil, produces deep purple plums good for jam or jelly.
    6 ft.

Juneberry *(Amelanchier canadensis)*. Fruit is similar in taste to blueberry, but shrub can be grown more quickly. Is very hardy and not fussy about soil. Red berries turn blue, are highly ornamental, and make good pies.
    10–12 ft.

Nanking Cherry *(Prunus tomentosa)*. Is very hardy. Showy white blossoms are followed by bright red fruit of true cherry flavor.
    8–10 ft.

Prunus Japonica. A dwarf bush cherry that is good for hedge or specimen planting. White flowers are followed by red fruit that make good jam. Two are needed for pollination.

2–3 ft.

Purple Leaf Hazelnut. Round leaves are a beautiful dull purple to brownish red. Is good for foliage contrast; produces edible nuts.

12–15 ft.

Rosa Rugosa. Has crimson-pink, semidouble roses; produces abundantly, blooms intermittently until frost. When planted 2 feet apart, makes a rose fence that keeps out intruders. Each blossom produces an orange-red rose hip — nature's richest source of vitamin C.

6 ft.

Scarlet Flowering Quince. Single blossoms of fiery scarlet bloom very early in spring, covering the branches. Leaves appear later with a dark, glossy green foliage. Fruit makes a tasty jelly.

3–5 ft.

Silver Buffaloberry *(Shepherdia argentea).* Thorny shrub with silvery foliage is similar to Russian olive. Is very hardy. Orange-red fruit makes good jelly.

8–12 ft.

Western Bush Cherry *(Prunus besseyi).* Hardy shrub has silvery green foliage. White flowers bloom in May. Purple-black, marble-sized sweet cherries are good for pies and preserves.

4–6 ft.

Wild Black Cherry *(Prunus serotina).* A real jelly tree! White blossoms in spring are followed by delicious black fruit in August. A hardy, rapid grower that is useful for windbreaks or as a specimen tree.

10–15 ft.

The olive shrub (this one Elaeagnus umbellata) makes a good windbreak, and its red berries are used for jellies, too.

Flowering Crabapples

Height

Cardinal. Has deep pink blossoms and spreading, semiweeping branches. Is loaded in fall with large, deep-red apples 2 inches in diameter that are sweet but with crabapple tang. Is good for jellies, jams, and preserves. — 10–12 ft.

Chestnut. From Minnesota Experimental Station. Is intermediate in size between eating apple and crabapple with a reddish bronze color, crisp, juicy flesh, and nutlike flavor. Is hardy and cedar rust-resistant. — 5–6 ft.

Dolgo. Is a favorite lawn tree, hardy, very ornamental. 1¼-inch fruit is rich red with olive shape. Is good for jelly and canning. — 4–5 ft.

Hyslop. Is lovely for yards and gardens. Brilliant red with juicy yellow flesh. Is good for jelly and canning. — 5–6 ft.

Royalty. Very hardy, originates in Canada. Has glossy, rich purple foliage, crimson flowers, and small, reddish purple fruit. — 15 ft.

Sargent. Is dwarf and spreading with pink buds, pure white flowers, bright green foliage, and small, dark red fruit. — 6–8 ft.

Van Eseltine. Is very hardy, has good foliage and pink blossoms. Fruiting. — 10–12 ft.

Whitney. Old favorite that is good eaten fresh and excellent for pickling and spicing. Fruit is large, sweet, juicy, and yellow with red stripes. Is a hardy and heavy bearer. — 5–6 ft.

Crabapple trees make spectacular spring displays, provide good summer screens, and later, fine fruit for jellies.

unattractive feature on your or your neighbors' land. There are varieties for many different climates and soil types.

Be *sure* to order one of the improved varieties, and, if you are ordering berries, plant at least three bushes to ensure the cross-fertilization necessary for good fruit production. Sometimes, as with blueberries, two different varieties are necessary to ensure cross-fertilization. To make this easier, many nurseries offer package deals of three complementary varieties.

Nuts

Large nut trees simply are not practical for the really small property — a "spreading chestnut tree" would take up too much room. But why not have its smaller relative, the chinkapin, a bush-type nut tree?

In leaf, flower, and sweet nuts, chinkapins are much like the chestnut but have the added advantage of resistance to chestnut blight. And they bear young, usually at 3 to 5 years of age. Chinkapins do well from southern Pennsylvania to Florida and Texas.

Filberts (or hazelnuts) are another possibility and make excellent hedges when grown in bush form. The term filbert is usually applied to domesticated varieties and hazelnut to wild ones. The European filbert *(Corylus avellana)* is grown extensively for its nuts. And although you need two to produce nuts, both can be planted in the same hole if space is really at a premium. *Royal* and *Barcelona* make good companions.

For a slightly larger yard, a Carpathian walnut is a good choice. *Hansen* is a naturally small variety that even planted alone bears medium-sized nuts of excellent quality. Pecans are marvelous for eating, but eventually can grow to 60 feet or more. However, the hardy almond ultimately reaches a height of only 15 to 25 feet.

Planting Edible Shrubs

In some sections of the country, early fall planting is best for shrubs because their roots grow during the fall and winter months and thus become established before the advent of warm weather. But, if you buy shrubs and trees in nursery-grown containers, they may be transplanted throughout the spring and summer if the plants are watered properly.

If you notice roots on the sides of the plant ball, make several vertical cuts with a knife to prevent the roots from continuing to grow in a circle.

Principal Nut Trees of North America

Variety	Years to Bear	Ultimate Height	Planting Distance	Range	Pollination
Almond (hardy)	2–4	15–25 ft.	25 ft.	Southern half of United States and Pacific northwest	Two varieties
Butternut (grafted)	3–5	40–50 ft.	40 ft.	All regions	Two varieties
Chestnut, Chinese	3–5	40–50 ft.	40 ft.	Where peaches grow	Two varieties
Chinkapin	2–3	10 ft. (bush or small tree)	10 ft.	Southeastern United States	Two varieties
Filbert	2–4	15–25 ft.	15 ft.	Pacific coast, north central United States and northeast	Two varieties
Heartnut	4–5	50–60 ft.	40 ft.	Northeast and Pacific northwest	Two varieties
Hickory (grafted) shagbark	5–7	60–80 ft.	40 ft.	North central and south central United States	Two varieties
Pecan (grafted)	5–8	60–80 ft.	50 ft.	Southern United States	Two varieties
Walnut, black (grafted)	3–5	80–100 ft.	60 ft.	Most regions	One or two varieties
Walnut, English (grafted) (Carpathian)	4–5	60–70 ft.	60 ft.	All regions	Two varieties or mate with black walnuts

Planting Container Nursery Stock

1. Slit the nursery can in three places through lowest ring to bottom, and carefully lift out plant.

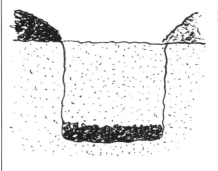

2. Dig hole twice as wide as root ball. Put some water in bottom of hole before placing plant in.

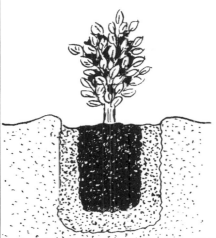

3. If soil is not rich in organic matter, make backfill mixture of one-third peat moss or compost and two-thirds soil and firmly tamp mixture around root ball.

Planting Container Nursery Stock (cont'd)

4. Water slowly, firming soil around root ball to eliminate air pockets. Keep plant at ground level.

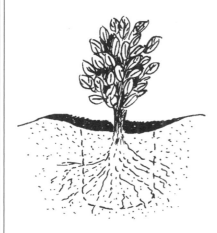

5. Mulch base of plant with 2 to 4 inches of bark chips.

6. Organic and other slow-release fertilizers can be added at planting time or shortly after. Other types of fertilizer should not be applied until the spring following planting.

Burlapped root balls can be left, but fold the burlap to the bottom of the hole after you have set the plant in. If the plants are bare-root, keep them wet and spread the roots in the hole.

Dig your planting hole twice the width of the root ball and about 6 inches deep. Keep the sides of hole vertical rather than slanting. Place enough backfill mixture (one-third compost, leaf mold, or peat moss and two-thirds topsoil) in the bottom of the holes and firm it so that the top of the ball is parallel with ground level; fill, tamp, and water to remove air pockets. Mulch with 2 to 4 inches of shredded bark, keeping the mulch layer thin at the base of the plant to form a water reservoir.

I cannot give exact rules for watering — your soil and the condition of your plants must serve as guides. Except during droughts, shrubs in most yards and gardens don't need additional water, but here are some points to keep in mind:

- ❧ Don't water until plants show signs of wilting before noon.
- ❧ Apply water slowly and thoroughly so the soil can soak it up before it runs off. Light watering encourages shallow root development.
- ❧ Apply from ½ to 1 inch of water per hour, according to soil type. (See Chapter 6.)
- ❧ Soil should be thoroughly wet to a depth of 8 to 10 inches.
- ❧ Water early in the day.
- ❧ Don't overwater. Under most weather conditions, one good watering of 1 to 1½ inches every 5 to 7 days is adequate.

Pruning Shrubs

Regular pruning, which makes plants grow or respond in the way you want them to and produces more and better blooms and fruit, is essential with landscape ornamentals, except for a few dwarf or very slow-growing shrubs. It also results in larger fruit.

Most spring-flowering shrubs and trees bloom from buds formed the previous year, so prune *only* after they bloom.

Pruning depends entirely on shrub variety. For example, Japanese quince, which produces flowers and berries only on branches more than 1 year old, should not be pruned unless absolutely necessary. Shrubs that blossom after June usually do so on growth made the same year so are best pruned in fall or winter while they are dormant. Evergreens grown for winter foliage, such as holly, should be pruned just before new growth starts in spring.

Cultural Requirements of Fruit Shrubs

Blueberry. Blueberries are great for hedges, and usually they need pruning every year to remove older and weaker wood. Their neat, glossy green foliage turns a brilliant scarlet and yellow in autumn. The clustered small white flowers, very much like the bells of leucothoe, turn to berry clusters from mid-July to September.

Blueberries prefer full sun and well-drained soil. You must have at least two different varieties for them to produce well. Plant them in the fall, as soon as the leaves turn color, or in early spring. Prepare the soil a little in spring, as soon as the ground can be worked, mixing in compost or peat moss. Note that the soil for blueberries should be acidic, between 4.0 and 5.5 pH. Never use lime.

To make a satisfactory hedge, place your blueberries close together — 3 feet apart in the row. *Blueray, Coville,* and *Jersey* are good choices for northern and eastern United States; in the south or southwest, where standard blueberries do poorly because of heat and alkaline soil, try the "rabbit eye" varieties such as *Tifblue, Menditoo, Garden Blue,* and *Homebell.*

Elderberry. This is the shrub to use if you have a partially shaded spot: Elderberry *(Sambucus canadensis)* is tall, vigorous, and spreading, with interesting compound leaves and large heads of dainty white flowers. It makes a fine screen because it spreads by suckers. Elderberry yields more berries if planted in full sun, but its one absolute demand is plenty of water before and after fruiting and is the perfect choice if you have a low, wet spot to fill. Keep the suckers trimmed at ground level for a fuller-shaped bush. Two improved varieties, *Adams* and *Johns,* bear larger-than-usual fruit. The purple-black elderberries (a good source of vitamin C) make wonderful pies and delicious wine and jelly. And you get a real bonus before the berries are borne: The profuse flower clusters dipped in batter and fried in a little oil are a delicacy.

Beach Plum. The beach plum *(Prunus maritima)*, which grows 4 to 10 feet tall, is almost the opposite the elderberry in its growth requirements and does best in a wind-swept, sunny spot where the soil is thin but well drained. In spring it is covered with many pretty white or pink flowers, and its purple-red fruit ripens in late summer. Prune it lightly to keep it within bounds, or it will make a scraggly shrub. Remember, you'll need two beach plum plants for pollination.

Flowering Quince. The flowering quince (it may be listed under Chaenomeles or Cydonia in nursery catalogs), produces exceptionally fine jelly fruit. The plants form large decorative mounds that need little care and, depending on the type, grow from 3 to 6 feet high. The various species have red, orange, white, or pink spring flowers. (A word of caution about quince: The double-flowered varieties are grown only for their beauty and yield no fruit.)

Bush Cherry. Bush cherries do not produce fruit as large as those from trees, but they are hardier and easier to care for. A bevy makes fine borders or windbreaks, or because they are self-fertile, you can plant only one.

I consider *Hansen's bush cherry*, an improved form of the Western Sand cherry *(Prunus besseyi)*, one of the best. It grows only 4 feet tall and makes a fine, low hedge. The Korean bush cherry *(P. japonica)* and the Nanking bush *(P. tomentosa)* are similar. All the bush cherries make handsome ornamentals, are covered with white flowers in the spring, and yield a lot of fruit for pies, sauces, and canning.

The shrub-like chokecherry *(Prunus virginiana)*, a member of the "bird cherry" group, grows well (to about 10 feet tall) from Newfoundland to Saskatchewan and southward to North Carolina and Kansas. The spicy, fragrant white flowers are followed by tremendous clusters of purplish black cherries that can be used for jelly and wine.

The Compass cherry grows to about 8 feet and is a cherry-plum hybrid that yields a good crop of bright red cherries the second year after planting. It is not usually cultivated as a flowering tree but is a useful hedge shrub that grows fast and stands clipping well.

The Sand cherry (see also *Hansen's,* earlier) grows in bush form. This drought-resistant, hardy native of the plains (from Kansas to Manitoba, Canada, and westward to Wyoming and Colorado), makes a good ornamental bush or hedge, and its black fruit (a heavy crop the year after planting), is good for canning or sauce, or fresh.

The Wild Black cherry, a hardy and rapid-growing small tree about 15 feet tall, is good for screening. It is beautiful in early spring, with great clusters of white flowers and, in August, bears a great abundance of edible fruit.

Buffaloberry. Don't overlook another native, the silver buffaloberry *(Shepherdia argentea),* which grows as a thorny bush or small tree, 5 to 18 feet high along streams from Manitoba, Canada, to Kansas. It is one of the finest choices for a shelterbelt or windbreak, and its silvery leaves and great ropes of bright berries make an interesting contrast among other plants and trees. The fruit can be used to make a very good jelly.

The buffaloberry is dioecious (male and female flowers on separate plants), so both male and female plants are needed to ensure fruit production. The species has no special cultural requirements, and propagation is by seeds, suckers, or hardwood cuttings taken in the fall and handled like grape cuttings.

Currant. Currants are easily grown in all the cool, moist regions of North America. Red currants are used to make jellies, jams, wines, and pies. White or yellow currants are usually eaten fresh. The golden or Missouri flowering currant, which grows wild in North America, is a popular garden plant because of its fragrant yellow flowers. Black currants are high in vitamin C, but be sure to plant a rust-resistant variety.

Currants are hardy plants and grow best in rich, well-drained soil with some moisture near the surface. Pruning the stems and shoots of this low, bushy shrub may be necessary, and all shoots over 3 years old should be cut away in the early spring, leaving about three 1-year-old, three 2-year-old, and three 3-year-old shoots.

Highbush Cranberry. This very desirable plant is discussed in detail in Chapter 12 in connection with mobile home plantings.

Gooseberry. The gooseberry makes an attractive shrub for lawn or garden and often is planted under fruit trees. However, picking the berries can be a thorny problem because the bushes are so well-armored. The improved *Pixwell* produces great crops of large-sized berries that hang away from the plant and are easier to pick, whereas *Welcome,* a new variety with light-green fruit that turns pink when fully ripe, is noted for its fine jelly or jam. European varieties bear larger, better-flavored berries, but the American ones are hardier and less likely to mildew.

Gooseberries, found chiefly in the North Central, Middle Atlantic, Rocky Mountain, and Pacific states, grow only 3 to 4 feet tall and do best in shady, cool, moist regions with well-drained soil. The shrubs can be grown from cuttings and do best planted about 5 feet apart in rows; be sure to firm the soil about the roots.

Juneberry. A North American native sometimes called snowy mespilus, serviceberry, shadbush, or Saskatoon blueberry, the Juneberry

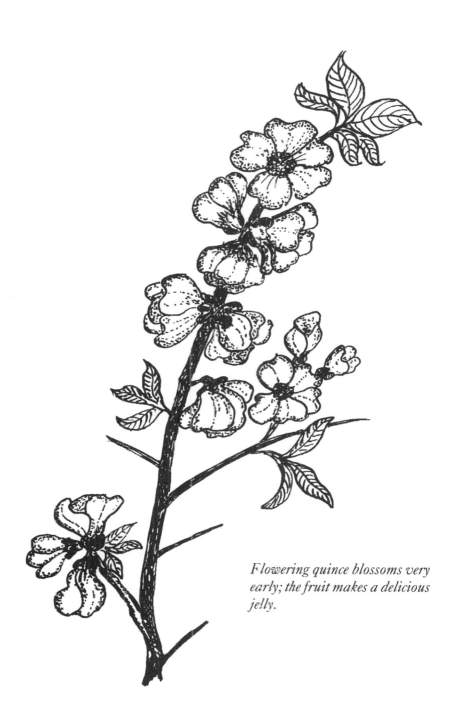

Flowering quince blossoms very early; the fruit makes a delicious jelly.

(Amelanchier) is a beautiful, hardy, spring-flowering, upright shrub or small tree. Its white blossoms in early to mid-May are followed by early-ripened, blue-black berries that look like big blueberries and are excellent for sauce or pies. In autumn, the leaves turn bright yellow.

The Juneberry, hardy and fast-growing, can reach 15 feet in height and thrives in ordinary garden soil, but it needs a sunny to slightly shaded location. It may be set out in early spring, but fall planting is preferred.

Grape. An arbor or fence in a sunny area is an ideal place to train a few grapevines. The leaves are beautiful alone, and clusters of ripening, fragrant grapes are as decorative in their own way as climbing roses.

Pruning is necessary from time to time and must be done correctly. *From Vines to Wines* (see Appendix, under *Other Books From Storey Communications You'll Enjoy*), gives complete information. Kniffen is the most popular training method, but other ways are used according to climate and location. The kind of grapes you grow depends on where you live. Consult your County Extension Agent to find out what grows best in your area, and choose from the good selections of hybrids available from many different nurseries.

Strawberry. No strawberries taste better than the ones you grow yourself, and even the smallest city lot usually has room for a few plants. Use them for low-growing walk or driveway borders if you have no other place. You might grow them in a strawberry barrel or jar, preferably one arranged to be turned so that all plants receive some sun. (If you live in the northern United States or Canada, be sure they are in a sunny location.) Here in the southwest, I plant mine so they have afternoon shade.

A new planting should be cultivated or mulched during the summer and irrigated during dry weather. After a hard autumn frost, mulch the rows with about 3 inches of a light-textured material; rake it off in the spring.

Summer cultivation is very important, and immediately after the berry harvest about one-half of the old plants that have produced their crop should be removed. Thin them with a hoe to a row of plants about 8 inches apart so that the new runner plants have room to develop.

Blackberry and Dewberry Types. There are two main types of blackberries: upright plants, commonly called blackberries, and trailing plants, variously referred to as dewberries, loganberries, and boysenberries.

Blackberries can be made to grow bush-like with side branches by

Keep border plantings of strawberries neatly in place by pegging down the runners with heavy hairpins.

cutting off the tops when the canes reach about 30 inches. This confines the plants to the row and makes cultivation and picking much easier. In the early spring, before growth starts, cut back the side branches to about two-thirds of their length. In older plantings, thin out the weaker canes, leaving three or four canes per foot of row. This pruning system improves the quality of the berries as well as the yield. These berries are hardy to Zone 4, but the trailing types are best grown in the southern and southwestern United States.

Dewberries require little or no pruning back, but do need row thinning and cultivation near the row to remove any tip-rooted plants. Work 3 or 4 inches of mulch material under the vines near the row during the winter for cleaner berries next summer.

Turn boysenberries' and youngberries' long canes or runners length-wise to the row when they are about 1 foot long to continue summer cultivation and make it easier to pick up the vines for trellising in the spring. They must be left on the ground during the winter to avoid winterkill, and if you live in a cold climate, be covered with a good mulch.

For clean picking, tie the runners on a wire trellis in the spring, but not until after the danger of frost is past, even though buds may have started to open and some damage may be done in handling. A two-wire trellis at each plant makes a good support for grapes, boysenberries, youngberries, or dewberries. Tie the canes to the supports with heavy twine or cloth.

Since blackberries and dewberries bear fruit on canes that grew the previous season, the old canes should be removed and burned after the berries are harvested. New canes will already be growing for next year's crop by this time.

Raspberry. Just as dewberries are fine for growing in the southern and southwestern United States, raspberries generally do better in the northern and eastern states. They often fit well along property lines or other narrow areas.

Plant early in the spring, using a good application of barnyard manure, if possible, and work the soil into a firm seedbed before planting. For a home garden, set the plants at least 3 feet apart.

Pruning is very important with raspberries. The red and yellow varieties should be pruned in early spring after frost danger but before buds swell. Remove all short and weak canes and then prune the remaining vigorous ones (leave five to eight canes per stake if you use the hill system). Prune canes again as soon as possible after fruiting. New shoots should not be summer topped.

Prune black and purple raspberries three times — in early spring, during summer, and after harvest. Dormant prune in early spring before the buds begin to swell. Cut out all weak canes at ground level, leaving four or five of the most vigorous ones (at least ½ inch in diameter) per plant. Remove all weak or dead laterals, and shorten the laterals of black raspberries to 6 to 12 inches of growth (or eight to twelve buds per lateral). The more vigorous purple raspberries' laterals may be left 12 to 18 inches long (or about 15 buds per lateral). In the essential summer pruning, pinch back all new shoots to 3 or 4 inches when they reach the desired height. If raspberries are grown without supports, this is when the black are 30 inches high, and the purple are 30 to 36 inches high. As soon as the berries have been picked, prune again, removing the fruiting canes.

Rosa Rugosa. The real secret of this rose is the rich vitamin C contained in the hips. The plant also lends itself nicely to hedge or specimen planting. Attractive single, rosy red flowers with golden centers in spring and summer are followed by large hips, ruby red when fully ripe, to be used for jam, soups, syrup, marmalade, and that delightful beverage, rose hip tea.

For a living fence, set the roses out immediately on arrival about 18 inches apart in a trench about 1 foot across and 1 foot deep, with compost or rotted manure below.

Rugosas need very little care, but cut them back to help them get established, leaving three or four buds or leaf nodes on each stem. After this, only cut out any winter-damaged or unwanted canes each spring. Place a thick mulch around the base of the plants.

You will want to pick some of the attractive roses, but remember that the more you take the fewer the hips. Gather the hips when fully mature but not overripe. If they are orange, it is too early; if dark red, it is too late.

The hips can be dried and kept for long periods and when fully dry can be ground into a powder. To preserve as much vitamin C as possible:

- Trim both ends of the hips with scissors before cooking.
- Use stainless steel knives, wooden spoons, earthenware or china bowls, and glass or enamel saucepans. *Never* use copper or aluminum utensils.
- Cook quickly, covered, 1 quart of hips in 1 quart of water.
- After the hips have cooked to the consistency of pulp, press out the spines and seeds by passing the cooked pulp through a sieve or food mill.
- For jam, add sugar and lemon juice; cook to 220°F.

Rose Apple. Also high in vitamin C is the delightful and winter-hardy rose apple *(Rosa pomifera)*, a pillar-type plant that grows about 5 feet tall and has beautiful bright orange hips about golf ball size — the largest produced by any rose species. The single-petal blossoms are a lovely shade of pink.

Rose apple, hardy even in the lower provinces of Canada, grows well in good garden soil and even better when pulpwood bark is used as a mulch and small amounts of poultry manure are used as a fertilizer.

CHAPTER 11

————— ✦◈✦ —————

Please Do Eat the Flowers

At the beginning of this book, I promised that on your small lot you can have a lawn and flowers, too — no need to give all your space to useful vegetables and fruit.

Of course, many of the dwarf fruit trees we talked about, especially the berry shrubs, provide colorful blossom displays. (And, don't overlook the ornamental vegetables, discussed in Chapter 12.) But, these handsome accents are limited mainly to the spring months. Also, their showiness is at eye level, which leaves your ground regions quite colorless.

Let's consider planting some appealing and fragrant flowers — those that also are good to eat, and not just in salads!

Borage. Borage, an annual, is easily raised from seed sown in spring in ordinary garden soil; the seedlings are thinned to about 15 inches apart. Seed sown in autumn produces plants that bloom in lovely, star-shaped pink, blue, and white flowers in May. You also may propagate the plant by cuttings of young shoots.

The leaves and flowers of borage impart a cool fragrance and refreshing flavor to tea and other beverages. The blue flowers sometimes are dried and used in potpourri. The young leaves also are used to give a cucumber-like flavor to salads. The flowers may be used as a garnish or preserved and candied by brushing them with egg white, sprinkling with sugar, and drying slowly. Steeped flowers and sugar make a borage syrup. Borage tea, delicious either hot or iced, is made from either dried or fresh leaves or flowers, or from the bruised seeds.

Carnation. Carnation usually is a greenhouse flower, but the clove or border carnation (sometimes called clove pink or clove gilly-flower), especially the variety *Dianthus caryophyllus,* is quite suitable for outdoor growing.

Clove pinks, as the name implies, are delightfully fragrant. The beautiful flowers may be candied as a marmalade, preserved, or even pickled with mace and cinnamon in vinegar. Minced petals are good in stuffed peppers, too.

The plants grow best in fertile, well-drained soil that contains some lime and in a sunny location. They are easily propagated by cuttings and by layering. Seeds give you plants that flower in 6 to 9 months, but considerable variation may occur because seedlings do not truly reproduce their parents.

Catmint. Cats love catmint (or catnip) leaves, and so will you in fresh salads, as a tea made of leaves, and with sugar to make catmint conserve. In my climate, catmint seems to grow especially well in the cool of autumn, and it is winter-hardy if placed in a protected location. Seeds sown in early fall produce white blossoming plants the following spring.

Chamomile. Chamomile tea, which so many know as a delicious and efficacious beverage, is made from the daisy-like flowers. It is also a very good rinse for blond hair.

Chamomile makes an excellent lawn in dry areas where grass will not flourish. Drought has little effect on its greenness, and when mowed the same way as grass, it emits a delightful perfume. To make a chamomile lawn, sow a mixture of lawn grasses and chamomile seeds. Because chamomile is the stronger grower, it eventually smothers the grasses, usually about midsummer when dry conditions prevail.

Chicory. The chicory flower, rayed and enchantingly blue, may be made into a conserve, like catmint. The roots sometimes are mixed with coffee or used as a coffee substitute, especially in the southern United States.

Chrysanthemum. Chrysanthemums bring bold color to your garden from mid-July until killing frost and come in shades of yellow, orange, red, purple, bronze, pink, or white. The long-lasting blossoms range in form and size from clusters of small, round pompoms to individual 4-inch decoratives. You can find spots suitable for small plantings of mums even in a minigarden.

Mums are easy to grow throughout the United States. They are sold in the spring as cuttings, in spring and in fall as packaged plants, and year 'round as potted plants. Well-rooted cuttings of hardy varieties quickly establish themselves in fertile, well-drained soil and produce underground shoots, or stolons, that enable the mums to persist from year to year without replanting. They need full sunshine all day in the northern or eastern United States; here in the southwest, my bed of mums receives only the morning sun and does beautifully.

The Chinese believe that eating chrysanthemums increases longevity and makes the body light and vigorous. Use the delicate, colorful petals in salads, in Oriental cooking, and even for an unusual creamed soup. The petals make a delicious wine; the dried blossoms may be added to tea.

Clover. Some people like clover so much that they mix the seed with that of lawn grasses. The plants are great soil improvers because they fix nitrogen by means of their roots.

Sometimes I eat fresh clover blossoms early in the morning when they are fresh with dew — you can actually taste the nectar that the bees love so. Red clover is delicious chopped raw and eaten plain or in combination with salads. Cook it also with spinach, turnips, or other greens. Chop fresh clover heads and mix with butter to serve on toast. Steep dried clover heads for a refreshing tea, reputed to be good for anemia or skin problems. Clover wine is delicious, too.

Daisy. The Shasta daisy, one of the best-known varieties of this popular flower, is beautiful for garden display and useful for cutting. It's easy to grow; thrives in ordinary, well-cultivated garden soil; and grows best in full sun. Daisy petals have been used in extensively in salads and for daisy wine since the 15th century.

Dandelion. My neighbors dig dandelions out of their lawns with a vigor and intensity worthy of a better cause, but I welcome them each spring, for the dandelion is deliciously edible. One of my favorite dishes is dandelion buds cooked with sliced leeks and seasoned with a lightly salted butter sauce. Or, try the fried buds in a omelette.

In northern U.S. areas, dandelion greens, either wild or cultivated, are an early spring treat. Pick them young, wash well, boil or steam, and serve with a vinegar sauce. The greens also are used to make soup or are mixed with other vegetables in salads, and the flowers are used for both beer and a very popular wine.

A thick-leaved type of cultivated dandelion is offered by both Stokes and Burpee seed companies. The hearts, when used as boiling greens, are greatly improved if they are blanched with the leaves tied up like endive. To grow cultivated dandelions, plant the seeds in spring in rows 18 inches apart and covered ½-inch deep. Thin the seedlings to 1 foot apart in the row, and keep the crop well cultivated. Don't let the flowers go to seed or they will reseed everywhere.

Geranium. If you have ever crushed a leaf of rose geranium (which is a good bedding plant), you may have noted the delightful scent. So, besides the colorful flowers, you can put the leaves to many uses — to make a delightful punch, a garnish for puddings, an addition to sugar for dusting cookies, a delicious butter, and a rose geranium jelly.

Gladiolus. Glads are attractive flowers that come in a wide variety of gorgeous colors, and the blossoms are quite delicious when made into a salad with lettuce and vinaigrette dressing. You also can use the blossoms as colorful cups for individual servings of shrimp or of tossed salads.

Set the corms of the small-flowered glads (in normal garden soil) 6 inches apart and cover with 2 to 3 inches of soil; plant the large-flowered types about 2 inches deeper and 8 inches apart. Stake the tall varieties. For a long succession of blooms, plant at intervals of a few days or every 2 weeks from the time the trees begin to leaf in spring until about 2 months before the first killing frost of fall is expected.

Lavender. Lavender is easy to grow and does best in a sunny, sheltered location on light, well-drained, sandy loam with compost or decayed manure added. It makes a good low hedge, perhaps to edge an herb garden. Most types can be grown from seeds propagated by cuttings or by division, as with chrysanthemums. In mild climates, the dwarf varieties are propagated by division in early October and planted in a cold frame or where they are to remain.

The delicately colored fresh flowers of lavender are delicious as a garnish for hot weather beverages, or they may be candied, pickled, or made into wine or jellies (in combination with mint). In our grandmothers' day, the flowers were traditionally steeped to make lavender water or dried to make sachet bags.

Lilac. The lilac, one of our loveliest flowering and long-lived shrubs, produces beautiful blossoms in early summer in various shades of purple

*Geraniums aren't just to admire.
Make some rose geranium jellies.*

or white that lend themselves to a confection called crystals of lilac. Flower fronds are dipped in hot water with gum arabic; next, in a mixture of corn syrup, sugar, and water; and then, sprinkled with sugar.

Lily. The daylily, whose abundant blossoms come in many colors from May to September, grows in almost any soil but thrives best with abundant organic matter. Although it will grow in light shade, a sunny location is best for most varieties.

The abundant buds of the daylily are very good to eat when dipped in batter and fried; the opened flowers also may be used. Asian cooks often add fresh or dried lily buds to soups, noodles, or meat dishes.

Marigold. I grow the colorful marigolds from fresh seed every year and everywhere in my vegetable gardens because they protect against many insects and, in time, control nematodes. Marigold petals, either fresh or dried, are delightful in salads, chowders, chicken soup, broths, rice dishes, or with meats, adding color and flavor. They also make an excellent flower wine. Marigold petals are good to feed to chickens and give their meat a tempting golden tint.

Nasturtium. The bright nasturtiums are another of the "protective" flowers to grow in the vegetable garden, or in boxes with cucumbers and tomatoes, where they are reliable insect repellents. (Note more data on nasturtiums' uses in Chapter 9 under Insect Protection.) Nasturtiums are high in vitamins A, C, and D.

Tender young nasturtium leaves are delicious used just like cress and lettuce in sandwiches and salads, or they may be pickled for snacks. The seeds, too, according to this 1871 recipe, are an excellent substitute for capers: Lay green seeds in salt water for 2 days; in cold water for 1 day; pack in bottles and cover with scalding vinegar, seasoned with mace and white peppercorns, and sweetened slightly with white sugar. Seal and store 4 weeks before use.

Pansy. The beautiful low-growing and many-colored pansies make practical and useful borders for walks and fronts of flowerbeds, and they bloom almost continuously if you keep them picked. As a bonus, the flowers may be crystallized, made into wine or flower syrup, and used in salads. The plants are very hardy but require plenty of water and not too much sun.

Peach Blossom and Plum Blossom. If you grow dwarf peaches or plums (see Chapter 9), you will have plenty of blossoms that can be made into syrups, conserves, vinegars, and butters. You can also make teas by

Pansies provide a colorful path border and can be made into a delicious candy.

steeping the fresh petals in hot water, or you can pickle the buds (see the recipe under nasturtiums).

Rose. The smallest property or garden is scarcely complete without at least one rose bush. Choose a hybrid tea or a climbing rose for a lovely screen. Many climbers bloom profusely and give you all the petals you can use.

Rose hips (see *Rosa rugosa*) are rich in vitamin C and as purée can be used in soups. Petals are good shredded in deviled eggs and for jelly or jam. From the petals you can make flower water (to flavor beets) or rose syrup (to flavor pork chops). Add a cup of rose petals to a cup of honey to make rose honey and use as a glaze for chicken, or to add flavor to carrots. Crystallized roses can be put into fruit compote.

Sunflower. Giant sunflowers can be important assets to the suburban lot, and their giant seeds, containing vitamin E, are very nutritious. Because of their fast growth, they are especially useful, as a temporary screen. I've even seen them planted in a square to make a children's playhouse!

Towering sunflowers produce delicious seeds for you and for birds. Eat the flower buds, too.

Sunflower seeds (also favored by birds and squirrels) are useful in cookies, candies, and other confections, but they are not the only edible part of the plant. The simmered fresh buds are delicious with lemon-butter sauce.

A violet-bordered path is handsome and also provides health-giving flowers.

Violet. Beautiful, fragrant violets, one of the best possible choices to border a path, driveway, or flowerbed, are also one of nature's best vitamin pills because of the amazingly high content of both vitamin C and vitamin A. Pennsylvania Dutch children have been eating them for generations.

Violets may be made into a syrup to use over waffles or hotcakes, or for use in gelatin. Crystallized blossoms may be made into jams and many confections, which may be incorporated into cupcakes and wafers. Violet water is sometimes used to moisten poultry stuffing.

The flowers mentioned in this chapter represent only a few of the possibilities for using dual-purpose flowers on a small property. At the same time, heed this warning: **Do not substitute the blossoms of just any flower for the recipes given here, for some may be detrimental or even poisonous.**

Flowers on the Table

Space does not permit me to include many individual recipes, but there are some general rules that should be followed when using most blossoms.

- ❦ Always select buds, blossoms, and leaves that are as fresh and perfect as possible. Never use any that have been attacked by insects or plant blight. And, of course, never use any that have been dusted or sprayed with insecticides.

- ❦ Once you have selected your flowers, look them over carefully for insects. Wash them gently in cool water, being careful not to bruise the petals. Place on paper towels to drain.

- ❦ If you are using buds and blossoms only, take care to trim off stems as closely as possible to the flower because they sometimes impart an off-flavor or may be bitter.

- ❦ If petals are the part to be used, trim off the white tips that attach to the stem, which often are bitter.

- ❦ Only enamel, glass, ceramic, or plastic containers should be used for cooking or storing flowers. Wooden spoons or spatulas are best for stirring.

- ❦ At certain times of the year, some flowers occasionally taste slightly acrid. If you notice this, add slightly more sugar.

- ❦ **Do not substitute any other flowers for those recommended.** Some are not only inedible but actually toxic. And do not experiment with wildflowers unless you are absolutely certain which ones are not poisonous.

Basic Flower Recipes

*(Use **only** the petals of those flowers noted earlier in this chapter.)*

Flower Water

1 pound of fresh petals with white tips trimmed off
Water
Glass or enamel saucepan with lid
Filter cloth or paper
Canning or other jar with close-fitting lid

Wash petals in cool water and drain. Place 4 cups of petals in saucepan and cover with water. Set over low heat and simmer about 35 to 40 minutes. Remove petals and add an equal amount of fresh petals. Do not add more water. Repeat until all petals have been used.

Strain liquid through filter cloth into glass jar. Tighten lid. Store for about 3 days before using.

Flower Butter

2½ cups of fresh petals, trimmed
Glass or ceramic container with close-fitting lid
1 pound of butter or margarine

Allow butter to soften at room temperature. Wash petals and drain thoroughly. When petals are dry, spread them in a thin layer in container; top with a 1-inch layer of butter. (Flavor may be intensified by using more petals and thinner layers of butter.) Repeat the process until all petals and butter have been used. Press down lightly.

Cover container tightly and store in a cool place (refrigerator is best if season is warm) for about 1 week before using.

Flower Sugar

1 pound of fresh petals, trimmed
3 cups of finely granulated sugar
Glass or ceramic container

Wash petals and drain thoroughly. When petals are dry, pound them together with sugar. (Use a mortar and pestle or an electric blender, if more convenient.)

Place flower sugar in container and cover. Tighten lid and store in a warm, dry place for about 1 week before using.

Vinegar of Flowers

2½ cups of fresh petals, trimmed
1 quart of cider vinegar (5% acidity)
1¼ cups of sugar
Glass or enamel saucepan
Canning jar with close-fitting lid
Filter cloth

Wash petals and drain. Pour vinegar into saucepan and bring to a boil. Add petals and sugar slowly, stirring constantly. Bring to a boil again and lower heat. Simmer for about 10 minutes.

Strain mixture through filter cloth into glass jar. Tighten lid and store in a warm place for about 1 week before using.

Syrup of Flowers

4 to 5 cups of dried petals
Water
Sugar
Enamel or glass saucepan
Canning jar with close-fitting lid
Filter cloth

Place dried petals in pan, compressing them as much as possible. Cover with cold water, 1 cup at a time. Bring to a boil and lower heat. Gradually add sugar in the proportion of 3 cups of sugar to each cup of water used. Again bring to boil. Lower heat and cook gently until syrup forms (about 10 to 12 minutes).

Strain into glass jar and cover tightly. Store in a warm place 10 to 12 days before using.

Flower Tea

Warm china or glass teapot by filling with hot water, then draining; place green-dried or fresh petals in teapot. Pour boiling water over leaves or flowers, and allow to steep 5 to 10 minutes only. Strain and use; sweeten with honey.

(Note: Adjust amount of petals used to individual taste, using more or less at the beginning of the preparation.) For iced tea, crush flower petals in an earthenware container. Pour boiling water on petals, allow to steep, and strain. Cover container and place in refrigerator.

Flower Honey

1 cup of fresh petals, trimmed
1 pint of honey
Enamel or glass container
Canning jar with close-fitting lid
Paper towels

Wash petals and drain thoroughly on paper towels. When petals are dry, pour honey into saucepan and place over medium heat; bring to a boil. Lower heat and add petals; simmer for about 10 to 12 minutes. Set aside, at room temperature, for 1 day.

Again place over medium heat and bring to a boil. Remove from heat and strain into canning jar. Tighten lid and store for 3 to 4 days before using.

Marmalade

½ pound of sugar
½ pound of petals, trimmed
1 cup of water

Crush petals in a mortar or pulverize in a food blender. Place sugar and water in glass or enamel saucepan and boil to a syrup. Add the crushed petals and boil very slowly until thickened, stirring well to keep from burning. Store in small jars, covered with paraffin.

Flower Soup

1 pint of milk or thin cream
2 tablespoons of flour
1 teaspoon of margarine
Sugar or salt to taste
Chopped petals, about ¼ cup (or use daylily buds)

Add 2 tablespoons of flour to ½ half cup of milk; stir until smooth. Place remainder of milk in saucepan, add flour and milk mixture and bring to a boil, stirring until thickened. Add chopped petals that have been soaked in boiling water for 2 minutes. Continue stirring for 10 minutes and serve while hot.

Flower Wine

2 gallons of flower petals
2 gallons of water
2 lemons
6 pounds of sugar
1 package of all-purpose wine yeast or 1 ounce of baker's yeast

Place flowers in a sterilized plastic or glass jug. Boil 3 pounds of sugar for about 2 minutes with 1 gallon of water. Pour over petals while still boiling hot. Add juice of two lemons and grated lemon peels.

When the "must" is lukewarm, add the baker's yeast or wine yeast "starter." Fit on a fermentation lock. Let ferment for 7 days. Siphon the liquid into another sterilized plastic or glass jug, leaving the flowers and as much sediment as possible in the first jug. Remove the flower pulp and wring out the liquid in a cloth to place in the second jug. Boil the remaining 3 pounds of sugar for 2 minutes in 1 gallon of water. Let cool to lukewarm and add to the must. Put on a fermentation lock and let ferment until all fermentation stops. Then siphon or "rack" into another sterilized jug, filling to the top so that no air remains in jug. Let "polish" or clear. When clear, siphon into bottles and cork.

Capers

nasturtium seeds, cowslip buds, or plum blossom buds

Take ½ pound of green seeds or flower buds and wash. Lay in salted water 2 days, in cold water 1 day; pack in bottles and cover with scalding vinegar, seasoned with mace and white peppercorns, and sweetened slightly with white sugar. Screw on lids and store 4 weeks before using. Makes an excellent substitute for capers.

To pickle young nasturtium leaves, gather when about half grown. If gathered in clusters, leave part of stem attached. Clean under running water and place in canning jar. Cover with hot cider vinegar (5 percent acidity), brought to a boil. Seal tightly and store for a winter snack along with other preserves.

Flower Crystals

½ cup of hot water
1 ounce of gum arabic

Make a mixture of hot water and gum arabic. Cool slightly and dip bunches of flowers (such as lilac). Dry on paper towels. Make a mixture of:

1 tablespoon of corn syrup
1 cup of sugar
½ cup of hot water

Bring to softball stage. Dip flower bunches. Drain and sprinkle with granulated sugar.

Crystallized Flower Petals

Egg white
Finely granulated sugar
Fresh petals (wash well and dry on paper towels)

Beat egg white until stiff. Brush onto both sides of fresh petals. Dip petals into granulated sugar (tongs make this operation easier). Put petals on paper towels and let dry completely in a warm place. Store crystallized petals in airtight container. Place waxed paper between each layer.

Rose Petal Jam

3 cups of rose petals, preferably red
3 cups of sugar
4 cups of rosé wine
1 bottle of liquid pectin

Mix wine and sugar in glass double boiler. Place over boiling water. Stir until sugar is dissolved. Remove from heat. Stir in rose petals and Certo. Pour quickly into glasses. Cover with hot paraffin.

Flower Jelly

1 pound of petals
1¾ pounds of sugar
¾ cup of water
1½ tablespoons of lemon juice

If using roses, select petals from those that are very fragrant. Be sure to remove white tips. Wash petals and drain dry on paper towels. Layer petals and sugar in glass saucepan, starting with sugar on the bottom. Add water and lemon juice. Bring mixture to a boil and simmer, covered, for about 10 minutes. Test by dropping a small amount of mixture into chilled water. When it forms a firm ball, remove from heat. Allow to cool; pour into sterilized jars and seal.

Flower Jam

1 cup of petals
1⅔ cups of water
2⅔ cups of sugar
1 package of powdered pectin

Separate blossoms from stems and discard stems. Measure 1 cup of petals or blossoms. Place blossoms in ⅔ cup of water in electric blender and mix until smooth paste is formed. Add sugar gradually and continue blending until sugar dissolves. Add pectin to 1 cup of water in glass or enamel saucepan and boil for 2 minutes. Add immediately to mixture in blender and blend well.

Pour into glass canning jars and seal. Store in refrigerator or freezer.

Specific Uses of Flowers

Crystallized petals. Use as confections or to top ice cream. Add to pies, such as apple or other fruits. Add to cupcakes and fruit desserts. Use to decorate pastries and desserts.

Flower buds (nasturtium, plum blossom, sunflower, cowslip). Use pickled and in salads.

Flower butters. Add to egg and fish dishes. Or use in cakes, cookies, and frostings.

Flower honey. Use for meat glazes (ham or poultry) and over vegetables or fruits.

Flower leaves (violet, dandelion, nasturtium). Use in fresh salads or add to stews.

Flower oil. Use in dips, canapés, meatballs.

Flower petals, minced (such as carnation or rose). Add to stuffed peppers, salads, and vegetable dishes.

Flower petals, shredded. Use in soufflés, deviled eggs, rice dishes, or over vegetables.

Flower syrup. Add to gelatin mixtures or as a topping for ice cream; good with waffles, particularly violet flower syrup.

Flower tea. Use dried flower of chamomile, dried or fresh rose petals, dried or fresh leaves of rose geranium, dried or fresh leaves and flower buds of lavender.

Flower vinegar. Use in dressing for salads or vegetables.

Flower water. Use in omelettes, fondues, meat sauces, vegetable sauces, stuffings, pie fillings, rice dishes, and marzipan.

Fresh blossoms (rose, elder, violet, squash). Use in fritters, puddings, or dip in batter and fry. Daylilies are particularly delicious.

Powdered blossoms. Add to meat casseroles, fish dishes, oysters, mashed potatoes, and cheese dishes.

CHAPTER 12

—◦━◁▤▷━◦—

Minigardening for Mobile Homes

Each year, increasing numbers of people, including many gardeners, are moving into mobile homes. For some, this may mean leaving a large landscaped site and moving to a tiny rectangle of land in a mobile home park.

There is no large lawn to care for any more, no big flowerbeds to weed. And yet, growing things was fun, too, wasn't it? And those big, crispy vegetables tasted so good fresh from the garden. When spring comes, you get the old urge again to grow something. But where (and what) can you grow in a minute space and perhaps in a new climate?

Check with the park manager to find out about rules and restrictions (and where utility lines are buried) before setting out with your shovel and plants.

Take note of any trees or shrubs already on your plot, and find out if you can remove any of them. Look at what your next door neighbor is growing, because you may want to try something different.

Perhaps you are also new to the area, not only having exchanged a large house for the easier upkeep of a small place, but an up-north home for a down-south one (or vice-versa). In this case, seek out the local County Agricultural Extension Agent for lists of the trees and shrubs that grow well in your new area.

Don't be afraid to try plants new to you, which may turn out to be just as attractive as the ones you grew before and in better proportion to your new surroundings.

A tour of landscaped mobile homes in your own and other nearby parks is a good way to see a variety of plants and arrangements. Large trees are out of the question, of course, but many shrubs may be possible.

Screen Plants and Edible Shrubs

Your necessary, but not particularly decorative, utility tanks might be screened with one of the viburnums with dense, attractive foliage and interesting flowers and berries.

Another good screening choice is the very hardy American high-bush cranberry. It forms a fairly large, open clump 8 to 10 feet tall, bearing white flowers in spring and blazing red berries with bronzy red foliage in autumn. The juice (which is high in pectin) must be strained and sugared to taste after boiling to make the jelly. Use the recipe for regular lowbush cranberry jelly in your cookbook.

Many of the other edible shrubs suggested in Chapter 10 also may be used for screening unsightly objects, for decorative accents or for marking boundary lines.

Vines

Screens and trellises planted with some of the edible vines serve to give you privacy from close — often very close — neighbors. The vines might be combinations of flowering climbers and fruiting vines, such as morning glories and scarlet runner beans. How about the other climbers, too: peas, gourds, dewberry, cucumbers, and nasturtiums, or perhaps clematis with roses?

Vegetables

Remember the big, vine-ripened tomatoes, fresh onions, radishes, and lettuce? If you're like me, you'd still like to grow a few of these vegetables. Well, you still can, and you don't need all outdoors to do it. Even if your lot is tiny, you can follow many of the basic techniques outlined in Chapter 3, making choices and probably confining yourself to low-growing, small vegetables and midget varieties rather than tall, spreading types. Depending on your space, consider making a planter box bed, as described in Chapter 2.

Basic Minigardening

Containers. The basic materials you need for minigardening are containers, seeds, and soil, including perlite and sand.

The size and number of the containers needed vary with the space you have and the number of plants you want to grow. Your containers should be large enough to hold the plants when fully grown. Six-inch

Beans and insect-repelling petunias make a fine combination grown on a free-standing trellis.

A planting of ornamental gourds provides a most decorative screen.

pots are satisfactory for chives, whereas radishes, onions, and miniature tomatoes *(Tiny Tim)* do well in 10-inch pots. Five-gallon plastic trash cans, half-bushel or 1-bushel baskets, if you have room for them, provide enough space for the larger vegetable plants.

Ready-made containers of plastic, metal, and wood — many designed especially for growing plants — are widely available, or you can improvise your own out of a pail, plastic bucket, bushel basket, or wooden box. Be sure to drill drainage holes.

There is no substitute for good garden soil (discussed in detail in Chapter 7), and for the super-intensive needs of minigardening it must be the best! For the limited amounts of fine loam or potting soil you need, a garden supply center or local florist may be the best answer.

Of the many seed varieties that are available, miniature vegetables may be the best to try. Write or call your local Agricultural Extension Service (this may be listed as County Agent or County Extension Center), for a list of the varieties recommended for your new area. When possible, select disease-resistant and insect-resistant types. For more information on minivegetables, see Chapter 4, Those Fascinating Midgets.

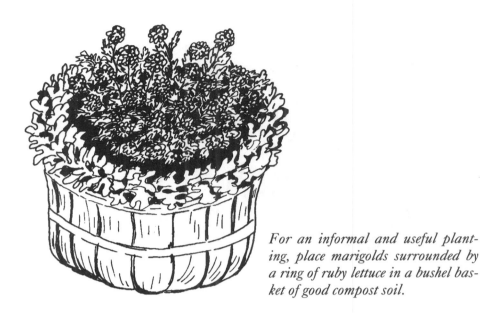

For an informal and useful planting, place marigolds surrounded by a ring of ruby lettuce in a bushel basket of good compost soil.

Light. When planning where to place plants, remember that although most vegetables grow better in full sunlight than in shade, some need more sun than others. Leafy types (lettuce, cabbage, mustard greens) can stand more shade than root crops (beet, radish, turnip). Root vegetables can stand more shade than vegetable fruit plants (cucumber, pepper, tomato), which do very poorly in shade. See *Vegetable Planting Guide* in the Appendix for more data on light needs.

Planting Dates. Planting or transplanting vegetables must be done at the proper time, but the best planting date in one area may vary by days or weeks from the best date in another. Your local Extension Service Agent can tell you the average frost dates in spring and fall for your locality and also give tips on other special area conditions and needs, such as watering, insect and disease problems, and controls.

Try 5-gallon pails (suitably camouflaged) as containers for tomatoes.

Appropriate Containers for Fruit, Herbs, and Midget Vegetables

Bean, bush	Planter
Beet	Planter
Cabbage	Planter
Cantaloupe	5-gallon container
Carrot	Planter, or several in 12-inch pots
Celery	Planter, or one per 6-inch pot
Chard	Planter, or one per 12-inch pot
Chives	6-inch pot
Corn	Large planter (hand-pollinate silks)
Cress	Planter or pot
Cucumber	Planter or 5-gallon container
Eggplant	Planter, or one per 10-inch pot
Endive	Planter
Garlic	Planter, or three in 8-inch pots
Herbs	Planters or pots
Kale	Planter
Lettuce	Planter
Mustard	Planter
Okra	Planter
Onion, green	Planter, or several in 6-inch pots
Pea	Planter (trellis for sugar pea)
Pepper	Planter, or one per 10-inch pot
Pumpkin	5-gallon container
Radish	Container that's at least 8 inches deep
Shallot	Container, or one per 6-inch pot
Spinach	Planter
Squash	5-gallon container
Strawberry	Planter, or one per 6-inch pot
Tomato	Planter, 5-gallon container, or pots (6-inch pot for smallest)
Turnip	Planter
Watermelon	5-gallon container

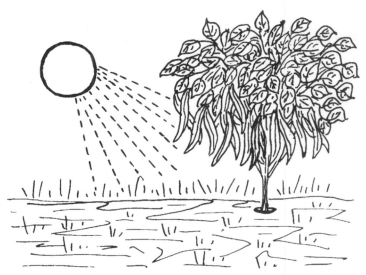

Reflective foil on the ground brings light and warmth under bushy plants and discourages insects such as Mexican bean beetles.

Ornamental Vegetables. There are a number of ornamental vegetable varieties that are pretty as well as tasty. Here are a few suggestions for your container plantings:

Flowering cabbage with one planting produces as many forms and colors as there are plants. Plan for late fall maturity, because plants need near-freezing weather to show their colors.

Salad Bowl **lettuce** produces many curled, wavy, bright-green leaves, and if you want color in your lettuce, grow *Ruby*. This beautiful, nonheading salad lettuce has fancy, frilled, bright-red leaves.

Two plastic containers with tight lids can yield valuable compost from kitchen wastes for the mobile home gardener.

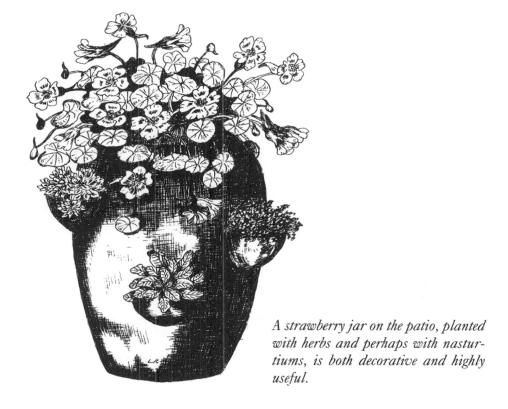

A strawberry jar on the patio, planted with herbs and perhaps with nasturtiums, is both decorative and highly useful.

Ruby Swiss chard is another bright-red vegetable; it looks like rhubarb, is easy to grow, and is very tasty.

Flowering kale has bright red-and-green leaves, or white-and-green ones. It is very easy to grow and is delicious.

Tiny Tim **tomato** does well in a 10-inch pot and is an especially colorful plant. It probably offers the largest edible return for your time and effort if you have a sunny spot.

Pepper plants are easy to grow and are very attractive, whether you choose the standard-size large green bell, the long "banana," or any of the smaller hot peppers, which can be dried and used during the winter months to add flavor to soups and stews.

Eggplants need full sunlight, and plenty of it, and are most successfully grown in southern areas. Their full-sized purple fruits are attractive and colorful.

Root vegetables, although somewhat less attractive to look at, can be grown in containers, and there are miniatures here, too. Onions, radishes, carrots, and beets are good choices.

Squash and **cucumber** need room, but still may fit in if the vining varieties are chosen.

Parsley, chives, and many other herbs can be grown easily in containers and take little room, or several can be grouped in one pot.

Strawberries, a surprising crop, can be grown in the confines of a strawberry jar.

Hanging Gardens

Especially where space is at a premium, don't overlook the possibilities of a hanging garden, both for decorative effect and edibility — tomatoes and cucumbers, for example, combined with petunias or nasturtiums. Or take geraniums, for instance. Besides the common type, there are peppermint, lemon, nutmeg, ivy, and oakleaf geraniums, as well as the rose geranium (previously mentioned), which has leaves useful for flavoring. Real strawberries, as well as the strawberry geranium, also may be good choices for hanging pots.

Take a walk through a mobile home park, and you'll see hanging gardens everywhere — under awnings, on step railings, and anywhere else that they conceivably will fit. They give more foliage and blossom for the space they take up than any other type of gardening.

Choose your containers with care. The best choices for warm or windy locations are plastic containers. Choose light colors because they help keep your plants cooler and retain moisture better than dark colors.

Containers always should be lined with sphagnum moss, then filled with soil. This spongy, water-retentive mixture keeps evaporation to a minimum. Even so, watering once a day may be necessary, and in very warm weather, take your plants down once a week and soak them in a tub.

Cherry tomatoes do well in hanging pots. Water them daily.

Container-Grown Fruit Trees

Dwarf fruit trees (see Chapter 9 for full details) lend themselves very well to growing in large containers. They blossom and bear fruit splendidly if tended with care and have the added advantage of being movable if you decide to change locations. Boxes of redwood, cedar, and other rot-resistant woods are best, but be sure that there are enough holes in the bottom for drainage.

Two parts good garden soil or loam, one part sand, and one part peat moss is a container mixture that holds moisture well and drains properly. Fertility **must** be maintained. Fertilize regularly every 2 or 3 weeks, or add liquid fish emulsion to your water about once a month. Water thoroughly until water drains out of the bottom of the container.

Tools

Mobile home lots vary in size. If yours is large enough, a small storage building for garden tools, lawn chairs and tables, pots, and potting soil may prove extremely useful and keep things neat.

Special Effects

Although mobile homes do have different exteriors, the basic shapes are much the same. Nevertheless, it is possible to make yours the complete expression of your own taste and preferences.

There are interesting ways to disguise the mobile hitch attractively, or even to cover it entirely (for example, with a small front porch). Another possibility is to work it into a small garden landscape, if the mobile home rests on a sloping area, by leaving the hitch flush with the ground.

Try a redwood planter box for a movable dwarf fruit tree. Keep the soil well fed with diluted fish emulsion or compost water.

A friend of mine disguised the motor hitch quite effectively by using the V-shape of the hitch as the frame for a small garden statue. The area in front of the home then was outlined with cement blocks and planted as a delightful salad garden. Two containers for tomatoes and several small, raised garden beds were placed on the east side for other low-growing vegetables. To complete the picture, edible and flowering vines were planted by the covered porch on the west, and hanging containers were added as well. Space was found in the back of the porch for a small dwarf fruit tree.

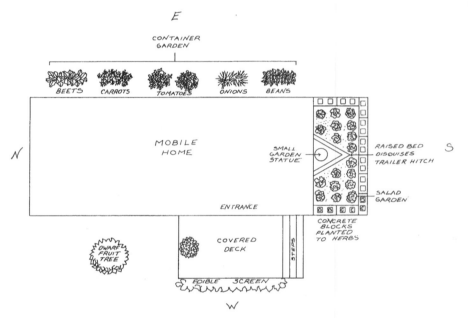

Plantings made around a mobile home can be fun and productive.

As the vegetables were used, others were planted, or flowers appropriate to the season were introduced. All of this made a tremendous difference — as only green and growing plants can — both in the appearance of the surrounding area and in the mental outlook of the happy owner.

You can use just about any material that is suitable to individualize your mobile home. While I was driving through a mobile home court recently, I noticed an extensive use of driftwood and even an old wagon wheel serving as an attractive background for a flowering vine. Cement

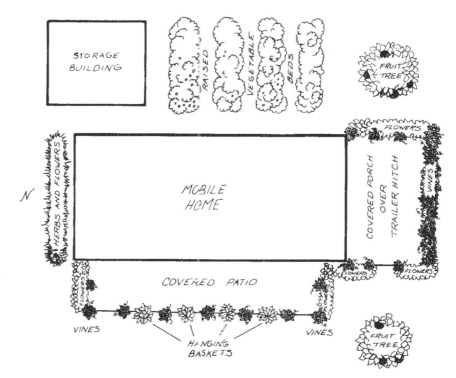

Mobile home lots that have more ample space can accommodate a wide variety of attractive beds, containers, and hanging plantings.

blocks were used as containers for flowers, herbs, and vegetables. Some shrubs and small trees were mulched with bark chips. Other areas were covered with marble chips, beach rocks, loose gravel, crushed rock, crushed brick, colored rocks, and various combinations. Plants were placed here and there in open areas of brick or flagstone, and containers of many types were in use on open patios and porches.

One home had a series of small, raised beds devoted to flowers, vegetables, and herbs, and the owner showed it to me with great pride. He was having just as much fun with his minigarden as the rest of us do with a larger planting — and he was harvesting a surprising amount of garden-fresh produce.

Although many effects are possible, I would caution you to avoid cluttering your space. A definite plan, neatly and carefully integrated and carried out, is perhaps even more necessary with the usual small rectangle of land around a mobile home than with a larger area. Plan on paper first, as I counseled at the beginning, and decide what you want to do with every inch of your property.

Just one closing word: This book has been great fun to write, and it is my sincere wish that the thoughts and ideas expressed will prove valuable to my many friends and readers. I hope that it will make your life more convenient, comfortable, interesting, and abundant; decrease your work and increase your pleasure in all phases of gardening. Happy days and success in all your undertakings!

Grow tomatoes, cucumbers, or a vining peach in a pot that holds its own trellis to screen the trailer hitch.

Appendix

Vegetable Planting Guide

Vegetable	High or Low Light*	Plant Week Before (-) or/After (+) Last Frost	Seed Planting Depth (inches)	Plant Spacing	Seed or Plants Per 100-Ft. Row
Asparagus (crowns)	High	2-	6–8	18 in.	65 crowns
Bean, bush snap	High	3+	1½	2 in.	1 lb.
Bean, pole snap	High	3+	1½	3-in. hills	½ lb.
Bean, bush lima	High	3+	1½	2 in.	½ lb.
Bean, pole lima	High	3+	1½	3-in. hills	¼ lb.
Beet	Low	2-	½	1–2 in.	1 oz.
Comment: Thin plants when 6–8 in. high; use thinnings for greens.					
Broccoli	High	2-	¼	18 in.	65 plants
Cabbage, early	Low	2-	¼	18 in.	65 plants
Comment: Can also be set out for a fall crop.					
Cabbage, late	Low	16+	¼	18 in.	70 plants
Cantaloupe	High	5+	½	2-in. hills	1 oz.
Carrot	Low	2-	¼	1–2 in.	1 oz.
Comment: To get several harvests, make plantings at 3-week intervals until 3 months before fall frost.					
Chard	Low	2-	½	6–8 in.	½ oz.
Comment: Only one planting is necessary; new leaves replace the harvested ones. Outer leaves may be harvested without injuring the plant. Each seed cluster contains several seeds.					

Vegetable Planting Guide (cont'd)

Vegetable	High or Low Light*	Plant Week Before (-) or/After (+) Last Frost	Seed Planting Depth (inches)	Plant Spacing	Seed or Plants Per 100-Ft. Row
Collard	Low	2-	¼	12 in.	¼ oz.
Corn	High	4+	1½	12 in.	¼ lb.
Comment: When tassels turn brown, watch the ears.					
Cucumber	High	2+	¾	2 in. hills	½ oz.
			5 ft. apart		
Comment: Needs hot weather. Start seeds in pots about 3 weeks before time to set out.					
Eggplant	High	2+	½	18 in.	70 plants
Comment: Hard to grow in northern United States because of high heat requirement and low growing season. Cover plants during cool periods. Start seeds indoors 8 weeks before transplanting time.					
Kale	Low	2-	¼	3–5 in.	½ oz.
Comment: Very winter hardy. Plant also in early fall for winter crops.					
Lettuce, leaf	Low	2-	¼	3–5 in.	½ oz.
Comment: Lettuce is a cool weather crop; it can be started inside early and set out even before frosts end. Plants tolerate temperatures as low as 28°F. Make several plantings for summer lettuce and in late summer for fall crop.					
Lettuce, head	Low	3+	¼	12 in.	½ oz.
Mustard	Low	2-	¼	6 in.	½ oz.
Comment: Can be grown throughout the summer. Make plantings at 10-day intervals for successive crops.					
Okra	High	1+	1	24 in.	2 oz.

Vegetable Planting Guide (cont'd)

Vegetable	High or Low Light*	Plant Week Before (-) or/After (+) Last Frost	Seed Planting Depth (inches)	Plant Spacing	Seed or Plants Per 100-Ft. Row
Onion sets		2-	1½	2–4 in.	1 lb. sets
Green	Low				
Bulbs	High				
Comment: Onions like abundant moisture.					
Parsley	Low	2-	¼	6 in.	½ oz.
Comment: Sensitive to heat. Parsley seeds germinate slowly; soak in water overnight before planting. Cover container for a few days after planting to keep soil moist. Start indoors if possible.					
Parsnip	Low	2-	½	4–6 in.	½ oz.
Pea	High	2-	1	2 in.	1 lb.
Pepper	High	4+	¼	24 in.	50 plants
Comment: Requires hot weather. If you start your own seeds indoors, plant 5 or 6 weeks before transplanting time.					
Potato, white	Low	1+	3–4	12 in.	100 seeds
Potato, sweet	Low	4+	—	12 in.	100 slips
Pumpkin	High	3+	1	2-in. hills	½ oz.
Radish	Low	2-	½	1–2 in.	1 oz.
Comment: Can withstand heat. The faster they grow, the better the quality. Fertilize at planting time. Radishes are at their best for only a few days, so you may wish to make several plantings at 1-week intervals. Try hotter, larger winter radishes, which need 75 days or more growing time and are planted to mature just before fall frost.					

Vegetable Planting Guide (cont'd)

Vegetable	High or Low Light*	Plant Week Before (-) or/After (+) Last Frost	Seed Planting Depth (inches)	Plant Spacing	Seed or Plants Per 100-Ft. Row
Rhubarb	Low	2		36 in.	33 plants
Salsify	Low	2-	½	2–3 in.	1 oz.
Spinach, hardy	Low	2-	¾	3 in.	1 oz.
Spinach, New Zealand	Low	4+	¾	12 in.	2 oz.
Squash	High	3+	1	2 in.-hills 5 ft. apart	½ oz.

Comment: Plant bush types.

Vegetable	High or Low Light*	Plant Week Before (-) or/After (+) Last Frost	Seed Planting Depth (inches)	Plant Spacing	Seed or Plants Per 100-Ft. Row
Tomato	High	3+	¼	24–48"	25 plants

Tomatoes offer a large return for a small space. They need warm weather. The Tiny Tim varieties can be grown in 10-in. pots. Larger types need to be staked. You may wish to prune them to a central stem and tie them up to a support.

Vegetable	High or Low Light*	Plant Week Before (-) or/After (+) Last Frost	Seed Planting Depth (inches)	Plant Spacing	Seed or Plants Per 100-Ft. Row
Turnip, root	Low	16+	½	6-in. hills	½ oz.
Turnip greens	Low	16+	½	3-in. hills	½ oz.

Comment: Turnips are a cool-season vegetable.

Vegetable	High or Low Light*	Plant Week Before (-) or/After (+) Last Frost	Seed Planting Depth (inches)	Plant Spacing	Seed or Plants Per 100-Ft. Row
Watermelon	High	5+	1	2-in. hills 10 ft. apart	1 oz.

*High light is more than 6 hours per day; low light is less than 6 hours per day. Even low-light plants need at least 4 hours of direct sunlight each day.

Vegetable Harvest Guide

Vegetable	Approximate Days to Maturity	Length of Harvest Season	Average Yield Per 100-Ft. Row	Processed Qts. Per 100-Ft. Row
Asparagus (crowns)	1+ years	8 weeks	30 lbs.	9
Bean, bush snap	48–56	2 weeks	30 lbs.	20
Bean, pole snap	60–70	6 weeks	40 lbs.	26
Bean, bush lima	65–90	3 weeks	20 lbs. w/pod	4
Bean, pole lima	65–90	4 weeks	40 lbs. w/pod	8
Beet	55–65	4 weeks	24 doz.	15
Broccoli	60–75*	4 weeks	40 lbs.	9
Cabbage	65–100*	3–4 weeks	85 lbs.	40 kraut
Cantaloupe	75–100	3 weeks	40 melons	—
Carrot	65–75	4 weeks	30–50 doz.	25
Chard	55–65	8 weeks	50 lbs.	30
Collard	65–85*	4–20 weeks	50 lbs.	30
Corn, sweet	65–90	10 days	100 ears	12
Cucumber	52–62	4 weeks	50 lbs.	—

Vegetable Harvest Guide (cont'd)

Vegetable	Approximate Days to Maturity	Length of Harvest Season	Average Yield Per 100-Ft. Row	Processed Qts. Per 100-Ft. Row
Kale	55–65	4–20 weeks	50 lbs.	30
Lettuce, leaf	45–60	6 weeks	150 stalks	—
Lettuce, head	75–85	4 weeks	75 heads	—
Mustard	35–50	2–3 weeks	40 lbs.	25
Okra	50–60	6 weeks	30 lbs.	9
Onion	100–125	4–24 weeks	50 lbs.	—
Parsley	70–90	6 months	15 lbs.	—
Parsnip	95–105	4 months	50 lbs.	—
Pea, green	55–70	2 weeks	70 lbs. w/pod	15
Pepper, sweet	60–75	8 weeks	400 peppers	40
Potato, white	90–105	4 months	60 lbs.	—
Potato, sweet	120*	5 months	80 lbs.	25
Pumpkin	100–120	2 months	100 lbs.	50
Radish	20–50	2 weeks	65 doz.	—

Vegetable Harvest Guide (cont'd)

Vegetable	Approximate Days to Maturity	Length of Harvest Season	Average Yield Per 100-Ft. Row	Processed Qts. Per 100-Ft. Row
Rhubarb	1+ years	2 months	60 lbs.	30
Salsify	110–150	4 months	20 lbs.	—
Spinach, New Zealand	70–80	2 months	100 lbs.	50
Squash, summer	50–60	4 weeks	70 lbs.	35
Tomato	65–85*	8 weeks	80 lbs.	25
Turnip, root	45–70	5 months	150 roots	—
Turnip greens	Thin early for greens	6 months	50 lbs.	30
Watermelon	80–100	3 weeks	20 melons	—

Capsule Information on Perennial Herbs

Perennial Varieties	Height	Uses
Angelica (A. archangelica)	5 ft.	White flowers, roots used as tonic.
Catnip (Nepeta mussinii superba)	1 ft.	Fragrant lavender-blue flowers, good in salads. Thrives in poor soil in sunny spots. Cats love it.
Catnip (Nepeta cataria)	3 ft.	Tea from leaves aids upset stomach and indigestion.
Chervil, curled (Anthriscus cerefolium)	1 ft.	Bright green, finely cut, aromatic leaves. Use for seasoning or salad.
Chives (Allium schoenoprasum)	1 ft.	Delicate onion flavor, pretty lavender flower heads good in borders. Use for salad, soup, to flavor cheese.
Curled mint (Mentha crispa)	3 ft.	Mint flowers grow on spikes above leaves. Leaves good for flavoring.
Horehound (Marrubium vulgare)	2 ft.	Steep leaves in boiling water for cough remedy.
Hyssop (Hyssopus officinalis)	1½ ft.	Young leaves fine for salad. Tea from the leaves good for colds or cough.
Lavender (Lavandula vera)	1 ft.	Dwarf, deep lavender flowers; lovely fragrance. Use for sachets to repel moths.
Lemon balm (Melissa officinalis)	2 ft.	Whitish bloom, lemon flavor, tea for illness. Attracts bees.
Lovage (Levisticum officinale)	1½ ft.	Use as a celery substitute. Aromatic seeds used in cakes.
Oregano (Origanum hortensis)	2 ft.	Flavoring for meats, tomatoes, spaghetti. Tea calms nerves.

Capsule Information on Perennial Herbs (cont'd)

Perennial Varieties	Height	Uses
Peppermint *(Mentha piperita)*	3 ft.	Confections and baking. Leaves used medicinally for tea.
Rosemary *(Rosmarinus officinalis)*	3 ft.	Hardy evergreen shrub. Pale blue flower spikes. Seasoning, perfume, and medicinal purposes.
Rue *(Ruta graveolens)*	3 ft.	Use sparingly in salads. Nice companion crop to repel insects.
Sage *(Salvia officinalis)*	2 ft.	Leaves used in poultry stuffing, to season sausage or cheese. Tea good for colds.
Salad burnet *(Sanguisorba minor)*	1½ ft.	White or rose flowers, is good for salads, cold drinks.
Savory, winter *(Satureja montana)*	1 ft.	Dwarf evergreen. Lilac flowers. Flavor and seasoning.
Spearmint *(Mentha viridis)*	2 ft.	Favorite for enhancing meats and beverages. Good in fish sauces and salads.
Thyme *(Thymus vulgaris)*	6 in.	Lovely in border. Seasoning herb for meat, fish, soups. Tea good for colds.
Wormwood *(Artemisia absinthium)*	3 ft.	Leafy tops may be laid along back of roasting goose to cut grease. Leafy tops good for fevers and rheumatism.

Capsule Information on Annual Herbs

Annual Varieties	Height	Uses
Anise *(Pimpinella anisum)*	1 ft.	Chopped leaves used in salads. Seeds in breads, cakes, and confectionery. Seeds steeped in hot milk are said to induce sleep.
Basil *(Ocimum basilicum)*	1 ft.	Handsome, fragrant herb. Used for flavoring.
Basil, dark opal	15 in.	Dense little bushes, lovely for border, are deep purple. Fragrant and flavorful.
Borage *(Borago officinalis)*	2 ft.	Blue flowers are decorative. Cucumber-flavored leaves are used in salads.
Caper bush	3 ft.	Flowers buds are "capers" of commerce. Pickled for eating.
Caraway *(Carum carvi)*	4 ft.	Fragrant seeds used for flavoring breads, meats, and liquors. Root boiled as a vegetable.
Chamomile *(Matricaria chamomilla)*	15 in.	Flower heads make sedative tea. Scented foliage.
Coriander *(Coriandrum sativum)*	3 ft.	Small white flowers. White seeds used in confections. Young leaves in salads.
Dill *(Anethum graveolens)*	4 ft.	Yellow flowers borne in umbels. Leaves and seeds flavor pickles and sauces.
Fennel, sweet *(Foeniculum officinale)*	4 ft.	Leaves used in fish sauces, salads, soups, and soft cheese. Bulbous root makes tasty vegetable when cooked.

Capsule Information on Annual Herbs (cont'd)

Annual Varieties	Height	Uses
Marjoram, sweet (Majorana hortensis)	2 ft.	Sweet flowers in purple spikes. Leaves used in sauces, meats, vegetables, salads. Tea for nervous headaches.
Parsley (Petroselinum hortense)	2 ft.	Leaves used in stews, soups, salads. Sauce for potatoes in melted butter.
Rocket or Rucola (Brassica eruca)	8 in.	Quick-growing salad plant.
Safflower (Carthamus tinctorius)	2 ft.	Oil from seed used for culinary purposes. Infusion of flowers used as a laxative.
Savory, summer (Satureja hortensis)	18 in.	Aromatic tops used for seasoning for meat, eggs, sausage, poultry stuffing, and string beans.
Tarragon (Artemisia dracunculus)	3 ft.	Tall plants are dark green. Leaves used for seasoning.

pH Preferences of Some Common Crops

Alfalfa	6.0–8.0
Apple	5.0–6.5
Artichoke (Jerusalem)	6.5–7.5
Asparagus	6.0–8.0
Avocado	6.0–8.0
Barley	6.5–7.8
Bean, lima	6.0–7.0
Bean, pole	6.0–7.5
Beet, sugar	6.5–8.0
Beet, table	6.0–7.5
Blackberry	5.0–6.0
Blueberry	4.0–5.5
Broccoli	6.0–7.0
Broom sedge	4.5–6.0
Brussels sprout	6.0–7.5
Buckwheat	5.5–7.0
Cabbage	6.0–7.5
Cantaloupe	6.0–7.5
Carrot	5.5–7.0
Cashew	5.0–6.0
Cauliflower	5.5–7.5
Celery	5.8–7.0
Cherry, sour	6.0–7.0
Cherry, sweet	6.0–7.5
Chicory	5.0–6.5
Chives	6.0–7.0
Clover, red	6.0–7.5
Corn	5.5–7.5
Cotton, upland	5.0–6.0
Cowpea	5.0–6.5
Crabapple	6.0–7.5
Cranberry	4.2–5.0
Cucumber	5.5–7.0
Currant, red	5.5–7.0

pH Preferences of Some Common Crops (cont'd)

Eggplant	5.5–6.5
Endive	5.8–7.0
Garlic	5.5–8.0
Gooseberry	5.0–6.5
Grape	5.5–7.0
Grapefruit	6.0–7.5
Hazelnut	6.0–7.0
Hickory nut	6.0–7.0
Horseradish	6.0–7.0
Kale	6.0–7.5
Kohlrabi	6.0–7.5
Kumquat	5.5–6.5
Leek	6.0–8.0
Lemon	6.0–7.0
Lentil	5.5–7.0
Lespedeza	4.5–6.5
Lettuce	6.0–7.0
Millet	5.0–6.5
Mushroom	6.5–7.5
Mustard	6.0–7.5
Oats	5.0–7.5
Okra	6.0–7.5
Olive	5.5–6.5
Onion	6.0–7.0
Orange	6.0–7.5
Parsley	5.0–7.0
Parsnip	5.5–7.0
Pea	6.0–7.5
Peach	6.0–7.5
Peanut	5.3–6.6
Pear	6.0–7.5
Pecan	6.4–8.0
Pepper	5.5–7.0
Pineapple	5.0–6.0

pH Preferences of Some Common Crops (cont'd)

Plum	6.0–8.0
Potato	4.8–6.5
Potato, sweet	5.2–6.0
Pumpkin	5.5–7.5
Quince	6.0–7.5
Radish	6.0–7.0
Raspberry, black	5.0–6.5
Raspberry, red	5.5–7.0
Rhubarb	5.5–7.0
Rutabaga	5.5–7.0
Rye	5.0–7.0
Sage	5.5–6.5
Salsify	6.0–7.5
Shallot	5.5–7.0
Sorghum	5.5–7.5
Soybean	6.0–7.0
Spinach	6.0–7.5
Squash, crookneck	6.0–7.5
Squash, Hubbard	5.5–7.0
Strawberry	5.0–6.5
Swiss chard	6.0–7.5
Thyme	5.5–7.0
Timothy	5.5–6.5
Tomato	5.5–7.5
Turnip	5.5–6.8
Vetch	5.2–7.0
Walnut	6.0–8.0
Watercress	6.0–8.0
Watermelon	5.5–6.5
Wheat	5.5–7.5

Note: Most of these nitrogen sources also supply varying amounts of phosphorus or potash. For example, bonemeal contains 24 percent phosphorus. *(Courtesy of Sudbury Laboratories, Inc.)*

Metric Conversion Chart

Dimension

1 inch = 25.4 millimeters, therefore:
_____ inches x 25.4 millimeters = _____ millimeters
_____ millimeters x .04 = _____ inches

1 inch = 2.54 centimeters, therefore:
_____ inches x 2.54 = _____ centimeters
_____ centimeters x .394 = _____ inches

1 foot = .305 meters, therefore:
_____ feet x .305 = _____ meters
_____ meters x 3.28 = _____ feet

1 ounce = 28.4 grams, therefore:
_____ ounces x 28.4 = _____ grams
_____ grams x .04 = _____ ounces

Weight

1 pound = 454 grams, therefore:
_____ pounds x 454 = _____ grams
_____ grams x .002 = _____ pounds

1 pound = .454 kilograms, therefore:
_____ pounds x .454 = _____ kilograms
_____ kilograms x 2.2 = _____ pounds

1 pint (dry) = .55 liters, therefore:
_____ pints (dry) x .55 = _____ liters
_____ liters x 1.82 = _____ pints (dry)

1 pint (liquid) = .47 liters, therefore:
_____ pints (liquid) x .47 = _____ liters
_____ liters 2.11 = _____ pints (liquid)

Volume

quart (dry) = 1.1 liters, therefore:
_____ quarts (dry) x 1.1 = _____ liters
_____ liters x .91 = _____ quarts (dry)

quart (liquid) = .95 liters, therefore:
_____ quarts (liquid) x .95 = _____ liters
_____ liters x 1.06 = _____ quarts (liquid)

peck = 8.81 liters, therefore:
_____ pecks x 8.81 = _____ liters
_____ liters x 1.14 = _____ pecks

1 bushel = 35.24 liters, therefore:
_____ bushels x 35.24 = _____ liters
_____ liters x .028 = _____ bushels

Sources of Supply — Plants and Equipment

Your local nursery or garden center is likely to carry a variety of plants and equipment. To order by mail or to obtain product information, consult the companies listed below.

This is only a partial listing. *The Complete Guide to Gardening by Mail* is available from The Mailorder Association of Nurseries, Dept. SCI, 8683 Doves Fly Way, Laurel, MD 20723. Please add $1.00 for postage and handling.

Allen Company
P.O. Box 310-N
Fruitland, MD 21826-0310
Small fruit trees

Burgess Seed and Plant Co., Inc.
905 Four Seasons Road
Bloomington, IL 61701
Vegetables, flowers, trees, shrubs, seeds, supplies

W. Atlee Burpee Co.
300 Park Avenue
Warminster, PA 18974
Vegetables, flowers, herbs, trees, supplies

Burrell Seed Growers Co.
Rocky Ford, CO 81067
Vegetables, peat pots

DeGiorgi Co., Inc.
6011 N Street
Omaha, NE 68117
Vegetables, flowers, herbs, grasses

Henry Field's Seed and
  Nursery Co.
415 North Burnett
Shenandoah, IA 51602
Vegetables, herbs, trees, shrubs, flowers

Four Winds Growers
42186 Palm Avenue, Box 3538
Fremont, CA 94538
True dwarf citrus (lemon, orange, grapefruit)

Garden Way Manufacturing
20 Gurley Avenue
Troy, NY 12181

Gardener's Supply Co.
128 Intervale Road
Burlington, VT 05401
Composters

Louis Gerardi Nursery
1700 E. Highway 50
O'Fallon, IL 62269
Nut trees

Gurney Seed and Nursery Co., Inc.
110 Capital Street
Yankton, SD 57079
Vegetables, flowers, fruit trees, supplies

Johnny's Selected Seeds
Department 172, Foss Hill Road
Albion, ME 04910
Vegetable and flower seeds

J.W. Jung Seed Co.
Randolph, WI 53956
Vegetables, flowers, herbs, fruit trees

Kemp Co
160 Koder Road
Lititz, PA 17543
Shredder/chipper, compost tumblers

A.M. Leonard and Son, Inc.
Piqua, OH 45356
Tools and equipment

Mantis Manufacturing Co.
1458 County Line Road
Huntingdon Valley, PA 19006
Garden equipment, supplies

Mellinger's, Inc.
2310 W. South Range Road
N. Lima, OH 44452
Seeds, plants, containers, tools, supplies

The Meyer Seed Co.
600 S. Caroline Street
Baltimore, MD 21231
Vegetables, flowers, supplies

H.F. Michell Co.
King of Prussia, PA 19406
Seeds, containers, supplies

Midwest Seed Growers
10559 Lackman Road
Lenexa, KS 66219
Vegetable and flower seeds

Musser Forests, Inc.
P.O. Box 340
Route 119 North
Indiana, PA 15701
Trees, shrubs, ground covers

Netafilm Irrigation
10 E. Merrick Road, Suite 205
Valley Stream, NY 11580
Drip irrigation systems

Nichols Garden Nursery
1190 North Pacific Highway
Albany, OR 97321
Vegetables, flowers, herbs

Nourse Farms
Box 485, RFD
South Deerfield, MA 01373
Small fruit trees

Park Seed Co., Inc.
P.O.Box 46
Highway 254 N
Greenwood, SC 29648-0046
Vegetables, flowers, herbs, house-plants, supplies

Pense Nursery
Route 2, Box 330-A
Mountainburg, AR 72946
Small fruit trees

Pinetree Garden Seeds
Route 100
Gloucester, ME 04260
Vegetable and flower seeds (in small quantities)

Seeds of Change
621 Old Santa Fe Trail, #10
Santa Fe, NM 87501
Organic, open-pollinated vegetable, herb, and flower seeds

Stark Brothers Company
P.O. Box 10
Louisiana, MO 63353
Trees, shrubs, fruit trees (many dwarf)

Stokes Seeds, Inc.
Box 548
Buffalo, NY 14240
Vegetable and flower seeds

Submatic Irrigation Systems
Box 246
Lubbock, TX 79408
Watering supplies

Sudbury Lawn & Garden
301 W. Osborn Road
Phoenix, AZ 85013
Soil testing kits, peat pots

Territorial Seed Company
Box 157
Cottage Grove, OR 97424

Wayside Gardens
1 Garden Lane
Hodges, SC 29695-0001
Trees, shrubs, flowers, small fruit trees

White Flower Farm
Department 115, Route 63
Litchfield, CT 06759-0050
Shrubs, perennials

Porter & Sons, Seedsman
2775 W. Washington
Stephenville, TX 76401
Dwarf fruit trees

Zilke Bros. Nursery
Baroda, MI 49101
Dwarf fruit trees, shrubbery

Mail Order Sources — Canada

Seeds, Plants, and Garden Supplies

Aimers Seeds
81 Temperance Street
Aurora, ON L4G 2R1

Aubin Nurseries, Ltd.
Box 1089
Carman, MB R0G 0J0

The Alpine Garden Club of
    British Columbia
P.O. Box 5161, Main Post Office
349 West Georgia Street
Vancouver, BC V6B 4B2

Butchart Gardens
Box 4010, Station A
Victoria, BC V8X 3X4

The Canadian Wildflower Society,
    c/o James French
35 Crescent
Unionville, ON L3R 4H3

Corn Hill Nursery Ltd.
R.R. 5
Peticodiac, NB E0A 2H0

Cruickshank's Inc.
1015 Mount Pleasant Road
Toronto, ON M4P 2M1

Dacha Barinka Seeds Ltd.
46232 Strathcona Road
Chilliwack, BC V2P 3T2

Wm. Dam Seeds
Box 8400
Dundas, ON L9H 6MI

Dig This: Gifts and Gear for
    Gardeners
45 Bastion Square
Victoria, BC V8W 1J1

Dominion Seed House
Box 2500
Georgetown, ON L7G 5L6

Elk Lake Garden Centre
5450 Patricia Bay Highway
Victoria, BC V8Y 1T1

Gardenimport Inc.
P.O. Box 760
Thornhill, ON L3T 4A5

Heritage Seed Program
R.R. 3
Uxbridge, ON L8C 1K8

Island Seed Mail Order
P.O. Box 4278, Station A
Victoria, BC V8X 3X8

McConnell Nurseries
Port Burwell, ON N0J 1T0

McFayden
30 9th Street
Brandon, MB R7A 4A4

Natural Legacy Seeds
R.R. 2, C-1 Laird
Armstrong, BC V0E 1B0

Pacific Northwest Seed Company
P.O. Box 460
Vernon, BC V1T 6M4

Pickering Nurseries Inc.
670 Kingston Road
Pickering, ON L1V 1A6

Richters
Box 26, Highway 47
Goodwood, ON L0C 1A0

Riverside Gardens
R.R. 5
Saskatoon, SK S7K 3J8

Rocky Mountain Seed Service
P.O. Box 215
Golden, BC V0A 1H0

Saltspring Seeds
Box 33
Ganges, BC V0S 1E0

Sanctuary Seeds/Folklore Herbs
2388 West 4th Avenue
Vancouver, BC V6K 1P1

Seed Service
P.O. Box 215
Golden, BC V0A 1H0

Territorial Seed Company
206-8475 Ontario Street
Vancouver, BC V5X 3E8

Stokes Seed Company
39 James Street
St. Catharines, ON L2R 6R6

Composters

Bonar Inc.
311 Alexander Avenue
Winnipeg, MB R3A 0M9

Century Plastics
12291 Horseshoe Way
Richmond, BC V7A 4V5

Dominion Seed House
Box 2500
Georgetown, ON L7G 5L6

Stokes Seed Company
39 James Street
St. Catharines, ON L2R 6R6

Wireman Products Inc.
5780 Production Way
Langley, BC V3A 4N4

Other Sources of
Information — Canada

Gardening Agencies

Canadian Horicultural Council
1101 Prince of Wales Drive
Suite 310
Ottawa, CN K2C 3W7

Publications

The Canadian Plant Sourcebook
93 Fentiman Avenue
Ottawa, CN K15 0T7

Harrowsmith
7 Queen Victoria Road
Camden East, ON K0K 1J0

Heritage Seed Program
R.R. 3
Uxbridge, ON L8C 1K8

Canadian Gardening
130 Spy Court
Markham, ON L3R 5H6

TLC . . . for Plants
1 rue Pacifique
Ste-Anne-de-Bellevue, PQ   H9X
    1C5

Other Books From Storey Communications You'll Enjoy

———◆———

Campbell, Stu. *Let It Rot! The Gardener's Guide to Composting* (Revised and Updated). 160 pages, paperback, $8.95.

Campbell, Stu. *The Mulch Book: A Complete Guide for Gardeners* (Revised and Updated). 128 pages, paperback, $8.95.

Cox, Jeff. *From Vines to Wines: The Complete Guide to Growing Grapes & Making Your Own Wines.* 288 pages, paperback, $12.95.

Editors of Garden Way Publishing. *The Big Book of Gardening Skills.* 352 pages, paperback, $18.95.

Foster, Catharine Osgood. *Building Healthy Gardens.* 288 pages, paperback, $9.95.

Franklin, Stuart. *Building a Healthy Lawn: A Safe and Natural Approach.* 176 pages, paperback, $9.95.

Gardner, Jo Ann. *The Heirloom Garden: Selecting & Growing Over 300 Old-Fashioned Ornamentals.* 248 pages, paperback, $16.95.

Hart, Rhonda Massingham. *Bugs, Slugs & Other Thugs.* 192 pages, paperback, $9.95.

Hart, Rhonda Massingham. *Trellising: How to Grow Climbing Vegetables, Fruits, Flowers, Vines, and Trees.* 154 pages, paperback, $10.95.

Hill, Lewis. *Cold-Climate Gardening.* 320 pages, paperback, $12.95.

Hill, Lewis. *Fruits and Berries for the Home Garden* (Completely Revised and Updated). 280 pages, paperback, $16.95.

Hill, Lewis. *Secrets of Plant Propagation: Starting Your Own Flowers,*

Vegetables, Fruits, Berries, Shrubs, Trees, and Houseplants. 176 pages, paperback, $14.95.

Hill, Lewis, and Nancy. *Successful Perennial Gardening: A Practical Guide.* 240 pages, paperback, $16.95.

Jacobs, Betty E.M. *Growing and Using Herbs Successfully.* 240 pages, paper, $10.95.

Macunovich, Janet. *Easy Garden Design: 12 Easy Steps to Creating Successful Gardens and Landscapes.* 176 pages, paperback, $14.95.

McClure, Susan. *The Harvest Gardener: Growing for Maximum Yield, Prime Flavor, and Garden-Fresh Storage.* 304 pages, paperback, $17.95.

Men's Garden Club of America. *A to Z Hints for the Vegetable Gardener.* 128 pages, paperback, $7.95.

O'Keefe, John. *Water-Conserving Gardens and Landscapes.* 160 pages, paperback, $12.95.

Osborne, Robert A. *Hardy Roses: An Organic Guide to Growing Frost- and Disease-Resistant Varieties.* 144 pages, hardcover, $24.95.

Philbrick, John and Helen. *The Bug Book.* 128 pages, paperback, $7.95.

Pleasant, Barbara. *Warm-Climate Gardening.* 208 pages, paperback, $12.95

Raymond, Dick. *Down-to-Earth Gardening Know-How for the '90s: Vegetables & Herbs.* 208 pages, paperback, $12.95.

Raymond, Dick. *Joy of Gardening.* 384 pages, paperback, $19.95.

Riotte, Louise. *Astrological Gardening: The Ancient Wisdom of Successful Planting & Harvesting by the Stars.* 224 pages, paperback, $9.95.

Riotte, Louise. *Carrots Love Tomatoes: Secrets of Companion Planting for Successful Gardening.* 224 pages, paperback, $9.95.

Riotte, Louise. *Roses Love Garlic: Secrets of Companion Planting with Flowers.* 240 pages, paperback, $9.95.

Riotte, Louise. *Sleeping with a Sunflower: A Treasure of Old-Time*

Gardening Lore. 224 pages, paperback, $9.95.

Rogers, Marc. *Saving Seeds: The Gardener's Guide to Growing and Storing Vegetable and Flower Seeds.* 192 pages, paperback, $9.95.

Rupp, Rebecca. *Blue Corn & Square Tomatoes: Unusual Facts About Common Garden Vegetables.* 232 pages, paperback, $10.95.

Shaudys, Phyllis V. *Herbal Treasures: Inspiring Month-by-Month Projects for Gardening, Cooking, and Crafts.* 320 pages, paper, $16.95.

Shaudys, Phyllis. *The Pleasure of Herbs: A Month-by-Month Guide to Growing, Using, and Enjoying Herbs.* 288 pages, paperback, $14.95.

Tilgner, Linda. *Tips for the Lazy Gardener.* 128 pages, paperback, $6.95.

Vargas, Pattie, and Gulling, Richard. *Country Wines: Making & Using Wines from Herbs, Fruits, Flowers & More.* 176 pages, paperback, $12.95.

Yeomans, Kathleen. *The Able Gardener: Overcoming Barriers of Age and Physical Limitations.* 304 pages, paperback, $16.95.

For information about these books or to receive our catalog, please call toll-free 1-800-827-8673 or write to: Storey Communications, Inc., Schoolhouse Road, Pownal, Vermont 05261.

Index

Boldface page numbers refer to charts; *italicized* page numbers refer to illustrations.

Catmint, 135
Catnip, 67, 135, 173
Cauliflower, midget varieties, 66
Chamomile *(Matricaria chamomilla)*, 135, 175
Cherry, bush
  chokecherry *(Prunus virginiana)*, 127
  Hansen, **118**, 127
  Korean *(Prunus japonica)*, **119**, 127
  Nanking *(Prunus tomentosa)*, **118**, 127
  Western *(Prunus besseyi)*, **119**, 127
  Wild black *(Prunus serotina)*, **119**, 127
Cherry tree, pollination, **116**
Chervil, curled *(Anthriscus cerefolium)*, 173
Chestnut, Chinese, **122**
Chicory, 135
Chinkapin, 121, **122**
Chives *(Allium schoenoprasum)*, 160, 173
Chrysanthemum, 135–136
Clover, 136
Cold frame, 37–38
Companion gardening, *154*
Companion planting, 1, *2*, 114, 138–139
Compost, 94–97
Container gardening, 154–160, *159*, 161, *164*
  appropriate containers, **157**
Coriander *(Coriandrum sativum)*, 175
Coriandrum sativum. See Coriander
Corn
  hybrid, 63
  seed, open–pollinated, 73–74, *75*
  sweet, 56
Corylus avellana. See Hazelnut: European filbert
Costmary, 67
Crabapple, flowering, **120**
Cranberry
  American Highbush *(Viburnum trilobum)*, **118**, 153
  European *(Viburnum opulus)*, **118**
Crystallized Flower Petals (recipe), 149
Cucumber, 56, 160
  Burpless, 60
  midget varieties, 66
Currant, 128
Cutworm, *61*

D

Daisy, 136
Dandelion, 136–137
Design principles, 11–12
Dewberry, 130–132
Dianthus caryophyllus. See Carnation
Dill *(Anethum graveolens)*, 175
Double digging, 24–26
Drainage
  air, 20–21
  soil, 18–20
Drip irrigation, 81, 83
Dwarf fruit trees, 6–7, 108–115, 161
  pollination, **116**

E

Edge garden, 33
Eggplant, 159
  midget varieties, 66
Eggplant lacebug, *61*
Elaeagnus umbellata. See Olive, Autumn
Elderberry *(Sambucus canadensis)*, **118**, 126
Espaliered trees, 114–115

F

Fences, 36, 50
  edible flowering screens, 52–53, 153
Fennel, sweet *(Foeniculum officinale)*, 175
Fertilizers. *See* Soil: nutrients
Filbert. *See* Hazelnut
Flower Butter (recipe), 143
Flower Crystals (recipe), 148
Flower Honey (recipe), 146
Flower Jam (recipe), 150
Flower Jelly (recipe), 149
Flowers, edible, 134–140
  recipes, 143–150
  using, 141–142, 150–151
Flower Soup (recipe), 147
Flower Sugar (recipe), 144
Flower Tea (recipe), 145
Flower Water (recipe), 143
Flower Wine (recipe), 147
Foeniculum officinale. See Fennel, sweet
French intensive gardening, 25–26

Minigardening, 154–164
Mint, 68
  curled *(Mentha crispa)*, 173
  Peppermint *(Mentha piperita)*, 174
  Spearmint *(Mentha viridis)*, 174

N
Nasturtium, 1, 114, 138–139
Nectarine
  dwarf varieties, 109
  pollination, **116**
Nematodes, 1
Nepeta cataria. See Catnip
Nepeta mussinii superba. See Catnip
Nitrogen, 90, **91**
Nuts, 121, **122**

O
Ocimum basilicum. See Basil
Olive, Autumn *(Elaeagnus umbellata)*, **118,** *119*
Onion, 55
  midget varieties, 67
Open–pollinated vegetables, 63
Oregano *(Origanum hortensis)*, 173
Origanum hortensis. See Oregano
Ornamental vegetables, 158–160

P
Pansy, 139
Parsley *(Petroselinum hortense)*, 160, 176
Peach
  blossom, 139–140
  dwarf varieties, 109
  pollination, **116**
Pear
  dwarf varieties, 110
  pollination, **116**
Pea
  early, 55
  edible–pod sugar, *34*
  midget varieties, 66
Peat pots, *73*
Pennyroyal, 68
Pepper, 159
  midget varieties, 66–67
Perennial vegetables, 30

Petroselinum hortense. See Parsley
pH, 86, 89–90 **177–179**
Phosphorus, 90, **92**
Pimpinella anisum. See Anise
Planning, garden site, 12–13
Planter boxes, 33–35, *56*
Planting guide, vegetable, 166–169
Plant protection, *52*
Plant spacing, 27, 55–56
Plum
  blossom, 139–140
  Hardy Beach *(Prunus maritima)*, **118,** 126–127
  pollination, **116**
Potash, 92, **93**
Potato, midget varieties, 67
Preservatives, 3
Problems, garden, **58–59**
Prunus besseyi. See Cherry, bush: Western
Prunus japonica. See Cherry, bush: Korean
Prunus maritima. See Plum: Hardy Beach
Prunus serotina. See Cherry, bush: Wild black
Prunus tomentosa. See Cherry, bush: Nanking
Prunus virginiana. See Cherry, bush: chokecherry
Pumpkin, Small Sugar, 50

Q
Quince, flowering, 127, *129*
  scarlet, **119**

R
Radish, midget varieties, 67
Raised beds, 4, 26–27, **32,** 99–100
  planning, *26,* 28–30
Raspberry, 132
Recipes, 143–150
Red spider, 46
Renting a garden, 4, 53–54
Reseeding, 74
Rocket. *See* Rucola
Rock powders, 97
Root vegetables, 159
Rosa pomifera. See Rose apple
Rosa rugosa, **119,** 132–133, 140

Vines. *See* Vertical gardening
Vine towers, 46, *47*
Violet, 140

W

Walnut
   black, **122**
   Carpathian, 121
   English, **122**
Watering
   amount, 82–83, 85
   overhead, 77–78
   root zone, 79–83

Watermelon, Sugar Baby (midget), 65, 67
Water stress, 80–81
Water use, plant, 83–85
Winds, prevailing, 13–14, 36
Worms
   Corn earworms, *61, 65*
   Cutworm, *61*
   Hornworm, *61*
Wormwood *(Artemisia absinthium)*, 174

Y

Yield, vegetable, **5**

12662